MW01008686

Training Needs Analysis Toolkit

Instruments, Exercises, Resources and Surveys

Sharon Bartram and Brenda Gibson

Human Resource Development Press, Inc.
Amherst, Massachusetts

Contents

Preface

The inspiration for this manual has come from many experiences: our work as consultants, and meeting training professionals in organizations and seeing their desire to make an impact, yet unsure about which direction to follow; our own experience as trainers, when a manual like this would have made our jobs so much easier; and our experience of seeing training and development issues sidelined because no one has made the link between an organization's success and well-trained people.

We hope that this manual will help you to put your training priorities on your organization's agenda and help you to identify realistic training solutions to improve the quality of the people you rely on to make your organization successful.

Sharon Bartram and Brenda Gibson

SBG Associates

Introduction

Whether you are an experienced or inexperienced training professional or the person responsible for "people" issues, making your training count is the way to influence the future success of your organization. In order to do this you must be able to match all training directly to the needs of the organization and its people.

This manual is intended as a resource for analyzing training needs, selecting training strategies, and developing training plans to meet the identified needs. It contains reproducible handouts and exercises (worksheets) for gathering and processing information about training and development issues within your organization. This frees you from the time-consuming task of formulating methods for generating information, and allows you to make the contacts and build the relationships that are so important for winning support for training.

The manual is more than a set of activities and exercises. It has been designed to:

- provide guidance about the process of training needs analysis
- show you how to transform information into training strategies and plans
- furnish a variety of methods for gathering information at all levels of an organization.

As well as helping you to establish whether people are achieving known standards of performance, it will also be useful to you and your colleagues when agreeing on and setting standards that might not already exist or might not be clear to everyone.

Finding your way around the manual is easy. Part One examines the process of identifying and analyzing training needs. It starts by explaining why this is important and by showing the triggers to analysis that are your pointers to achievement. You will find guidelines for using the activities to best effect, including how to prepare your target groups, ensuring your success in gathering the information.

Part One also reviews the different types of information the activities will generate and lists the questions to ask to determine the appropriate training needs. A section on the benefits and potential problems of the primary training strategies will help you to decide how the training needs can best be met. This part finishes with ideas for presenting training plans, including exercises used by trainers that will help you to make your training needs analysis findings and proposals accessible to others.

Part Two comprises the activities, 22 in all. They cover:

- developing the organization
- organizational climate
- managing resources
- job skills.

Each section begins with an introduction, which defines the area covered by the section, names and describes the activities, and identifies the target groups. It also provides a checklist of the preparations you must make in order to achieve success. Each activity conforms to a standard layout, making it easy to follow. You will always be given:

- the purpose of the activity — what it is intended to do
- a description of the activity — the format it takes
- the materials you require.

Most of the activities also explain methods for collecting information, with clear steps for administering the activity, whether it is by mail, individual interviews, group discussions, and so on. The merits of each method are explained as well as some of the potential problems that are worth thinking about before you make a choice. This helps you to select the activity most appropriate to your needs and the best way of using it with your intended target group.

When you read through the sections you will see that the activities present a wide range of methods, including card sorts, questionnaires, profiles, and grids. This diversity has two important advantages: first, training needs analysis does not have to be repetitive and boring; and second, if you find a method that works well in your organization, such as the card sort, you could adapt some of the other activities to this approach. Questionnaires, for example, can be adapted quickly by putting each question on a separate card. This adaptability ensures that you will find the most appropriate way to generate the information you are looking for.

Training and development requires investment in time and finance. Even with an analysis of training needs and development of plans that address these needs, the unexpected can occur. Sometimes this is because of issues outside your control and other times it is because the training approach is still not the solution for the need. The best approach is to be prepared to monitor progress constantly and to make plans that are realistic and achievable. This manual will help you to carry out effective training needs analyses so that the investment your organization makes will achieve the desired results.

Symbols for Activities

✏️ **Trainer's Guide**

? **Exercise**

PART ONE

Analyzing Training Needs

Why Analyze Training Needs?

Analyzing training needs provides a focus and direction for the investment an organization has to make in its people. Some training needs are obvious:

- Beginners with little or no experience of the job they have been recruited to do will not be able to make a positive contribution until they have acquired the knowledge and skills of their job.
- Newly appointed first-line managers may have excellent job skills — that could be the reason for their promotion — but they will only obtain the best from the team when they have had the opportunity to develop their "people management" skills.

Even when training needs appear to be obvious, it is still necessary to analyze the specific knowledge and skill requirements in order to choose appropriate methods that will meet them. The new manager requires an individual plan showing the sequence of training, who the trainer will be, and how the training will be delivered. We know that the newly appointed manager should have people management skills, but what are the priorities? Is it leadership, team building or perhaps communications skills? Without the benefit of further analysis, it is easy to see how time and finances can be invested in the wrong areas. What are the consequences of this? Training costs money but does not add value to the organization if the people are not being developed in the best way.

Many training needs are not obvious. Think about those people who have been doing their jobs for a long time and are competent at what they do. By analyzing their performance you could identify aspects that could be improved or you might find potential that is not being fully developed.

When new systems or methods of working are introduced, is enough thought given to the impact they will have on people? Without analyzing the changes the new systems and methods will mean to the jobs people do, it will be difficult to prepare your work force to adapt to new knowledge and skill requirements.

Much emphasis is placed these days on organizations going through a strategic planning phase, developing business plans and forecasts to set targets for their future growth. How many organizations find out if their work force is capable of achieving the new and different goals this growth will demand? By analyzing the current capabilities of people, it is much easier to predict and overcome the potential barriers to achieving the targets set.

Because training and development is an investment, it is important to treat it as seriously as an investment made, in machinery, new technology, or the physical premises. Determining the benefits in comparison to costs is just as important in the training and development area. An effective training needs analysis will contribute to this by identifying training issues and priorities in a systematic way, not on an ad hoc basis. By examining individual as well as overall aspects of the organization, effective decisions can be made.

Thus, the benefits to you and your organization can be that:

- Investment in training and development will have a focus and direction.
- Priority training needs throughout the organization will become apparent.
- Appropriate methods for meeting these needs will be identified.
- Training will be systematic and planned but flexible enough to cope with ad hoc requests.
- The benefits of training will be measured against the initial costs.
- The contribution training makes to organizational growth and success will be recognized.

The consequences of not carrying out a detailed analysis of training needs are the negatives of the above benefits. Whether you and your organization are in a time of boom or recession, can you afford to risk your investment in this way? The people who pay the price ultimately are the employees who, without the right training and development, can be your biggest liability. With effective training, however, they can become your biggest asset.

Starting Your Analysis

In order to begin your training needs analysis, ask yourself the questions given below. Under the "Notes" column, suggested action steps are occasionally provided. Use this space for your own thoughts and ideas too.

Questions	*Notes*

• What is happening in your organization that might be a trigger for a training needs analysis? Potential triggers might include:
 	
  – taking on new people
  – internal promotions or transfers
  – new procedures and systems
  – new standards
  – new structures and relationships
  – new products
  – new customers
  – new equipment
  – appraisals
  – requests from your manager, senior managers, individuals
  – review of previous training plans	

• Are there any negative indicators in your organization that might be additional triggers? Negative indicators might include:
 	
  – customer complaints
  – accident records
  – increasing numbers of grievance and/or disciplinary situations
  – high turnover of new recruits
  – loss of customers
  – increasing turnover of experienced employees
  – disputes
  – standards of work not being achieved
	Look out for links between the triggers. For example, could the increase in turnover of experienced employees be having an effect on loss of customers? Add to this the new recruits and it is likely there is increasing pressure on managers. Perhaps this is affecting how they manage. Look at the increase in disciplinary matters and check appraisals for comments about this.

• What external influences are there on your organization that might be further triggers? External indicators might include:
 	
  – new legislation
  – changes to legislation
  – customer requirements
  – competitor activity
  – supplier activity	

Questions	Notes

• Who is likely to be affected by each of these triggers
 	
   – the people at the top?
   – senior managers of functions?
   – departmental managers?
   – section managers, supervisors?
   – other grades, such as clerical, operational?
	Create a matrix to show the match between the triggers and the people most likely to be affected.

• Where can you find information about these triggers? For example:
 	
   – training records
   – personal records
   – health and safety audits
   – sales figures
   – management information
   – appraisal documentation
	Make a list of all the potential sources of information under the categories of documents, records, people, to speed up the retrieval of the details.

Identifying the triggers in this way is an important first step toward an effective training needs analysis. It will give you an overall impression of what is happening around you, but do not jump to conclusions at this point about what training is required. For example, one company who telephoned customers for debt collections and experienced poor results saw the need for effective telephone training. Although an investment was made in what was thought to be better training, the situation did not improve. This time they analyzed exactly what people were doing and found that the real training need was for debt collecting skills. The investment paid off when the trigger changed.

So far you have only considered indicators and their function has been to give direction to your analysis. This focus enables you to plan what you have to find out, which activity or combination of activities will give you this information, and the people with whom you want to use the activity. With some triggers it is worth using more than one activity to generate information about the issue from as many different perspectives as possible. An example is the company for whom a powerful trigger was the desire to improve their competitiveness. They could have used Activity 3 (p. 37) in the section on "Developing the Organization." In fact, by combining this activity with the one on customer needs (see Activity 5, p. 49) in the same section together with the work fulfillment activity (p. 67, Activity 7) from the section on "Organizational Climate" they obtained a comprehensive picture of their strengths and weaknesses, what their customers thought about them, and how motivated their employees were. By identifying what needed to be done and the consequent training implications the company was more likely to realize its ambition of improving competitiveness.

You must also decide whether you require a sponsor or champion to commit to the analysis or is there one already who is pushing for action? If you have to find a sponsor or champion, carefully determine the most appropriate person. It must be someone with sufficient authority to sanction training expenditure and who is capable of influencing others who may not give their full support. You must be sure you have their backing before embarking on a training needs analysis as this type of activity always raises people's expectations. You will do more harm than good if you undertake an analysis, identify a training need, and implement a training plan without this support. Think of the manager in one organization who felt strongly that there was a need for training in decision-making skills. The manager organized and ran the first in a series of courses, and was reprimanded by the chief executive for wasting time and money. In the chief executive's eyes, training in decision-making skills was not a priority, so it was brought to a halt. Such disasters take a long time to recover from and may damage the contribution training can make to an organization.

Additionally, the triggers will indicate whether your analysis will cover areas where standards are clearly defined, such as job skills and managing resources (Activities 11–22), or where they do not exist or are not formulated, such as developing the organization and organizational climate (Activities 1–10). These are not hard and fast categories but form a general rule.

Use the layout in Table A (p. 18) as a way of making notes about these issues for yourself. Keep a master of the layout and photocopy it each time you carry out an analysis.

Using the Activities

When you begin to use the activities, and in order to use them effectively, you must first accurately identify the target group and then explain the purpose of the activity to them. As a general rule, the people with whom you will use the activities follow the pattern in the matrix on page 18.

Once you have identified these people, you can prepare them for using the activities. It is best to do this in a face-to-face meeting so that you can allay any fears individuals might have about the consequences of taking part in the analysis. This will avoid the following scenario presented as an example. An organization invited a group of managers to a training course and used it as an opportunity to carry out a training needs analysis. It seemed a good idea to send out a self-assessment questionnaire with the course instructions but, in reality, most of the managers were alarmed that if they could not do everything suggested by the questionnaire they would be disciplined or, worse, dismissed! This highlights the way people were managed in that organization and so you must also be aware of the barriers people might be facing within your own organization. Setting aside time for a face-to-face meeting, on a

Index of Activities

Target Groups

Activity	People at the top of the organization: • managing directors • general managers or equivalents	People who manage others: • senior managers of functions • departmental managers • section managers • supervisors or equivalents	People who do not manage others: • clerical • technical • manual or equivalents
1. Focus on Perceptions	•		
2. Measures of Success	•		
3. Organizational Profile	•		
4. Defining Excellence	•		
5. Customer Satisfaction	•		
6. Communications	•	•	•
7. Work Fulfillment		•	•
8. What Drives This Organization?	•	•	•
9. Evidence of Equality	•	•	•
10. Is This a Learning Organization?	•	•	•
11. Personal Assessment		•	
12. Management Match		•	
13. Managing Time		•	
14. Managing People		•	
15. Managing Expenditure		•	
16. How Others See Me	•	•	•
17. How Do I See My Managers?	•	•	
18. Analyzing Jobs		•	•
19. Training Needs Survey		•	•
20. Task Competencies		•	•
21. Working with Others		•	•
22. Skills Questionaire		•	•

one-to-one or group basis, will help you overcome these issues. The areas you should cover during this meeting are shown below, with space for you to make notes about your ideas.

Meeting content	*Notes*
• Define training needs analysis for the group. • Ask the group's previous experience of training needs analysis. • Explain the background to this training needs analysis. • Clarify the group's involvement. • Stress why this is important. • Discuss the benefits to them of carrying this out. • Display the worksheet. • Explain what it sets out to achieve. • Allow time for questions. • Explain how their information will be used. • Stress the positive nature of training needs analysis. • Check for understanding of what is expected of them. • Explain what will happen after the briefing.	

As you begin to use the activities more regularly you will find it helpful to monitor the success of the different methods they offer you. The method itself, whether it is a card sort or a questionnaire, may not suit the people using it. You must take account of the type of organization you work for, what people are used to, the systems you have in place and so on. There will be some organizations who are used to dealing with paperwork, who like to generate reports, and where responding to questionnaires would be very acceptable, but taking part in discussion groups might be less suitable. There will be others who communicate verbally, with less emphasis on paperwork, and who like to be creative. Here, card sorts and brainstorming would be more effective than questionnaires and profiles. Think about the type of organization that you are in and keep a log of what produces the best responses. Work out how to prepare people for practices that may be new to them and how to adapt the instruments to meet your needs more closely. A suggested layout for your log is shown in Table B (p. 19).

Your familiarity with the activities will also enable you to take advantage of further ideas which may spring from them. For example you could use some of the activities as a basis for:

- one-to-one coaching
- discussion groups
- training course objectives
- training course content.

They also represent learning opportunities in themselves. For example, anyone using Activity 11, "Personal Assessment," in the section about managing resources will have already become aware of how they are using their time at work.

Open your mind to the possibilities created by using the activities so that the effort you and your organization put into them is worthwhile, thus generating quality information from which to develop successful strategies and plans.

Type of Information Gathered

As you read through the activities you will see that each section serves a different purpose.

(A) Developing the organization — where the organization is now, where it sees itself in the future, and the necessary changes you will have to make. The information generated by the activities will describe these changes and the appropriate actions to achieve them.

(B) Organizational climate — helps you to take the temperature of the organization, finding out about people's perceptions of what is happening around them, how they are treated, and so on. The information generated by these activities will be a collection of these views and will form the basis for discussion with the people at the top of the organization.

(C) Managing resources — the styles and levels of competence the managers currently possess, usually comparing these to best management practice. The information generated by these activities will show how closely the managers' skills match the best practice and identify areas for development.

(D) Job skills — the entire range of knowledge, practical skills, and behavioral skills required by people to do their jobs. The activities help to clarify what they are, who possesses them, and who needs to develop them. They also offer an opportunity to discover talent and skills that are underutilized. The information generated shows the range of knowledge and skills among the cross section of people, highlighting areas for action.

Questions	Y	N	Responses
Does the change/action imply new systems, procedures, etc?	✓		If they fundamentally alter how people do their jobs, it is likely that some training will be necessary to use the new systems and procedures. Look at Activities 18–22 to find out what people already do before making a final decision.
Does the change/action imply new or revised job responsibilities?	✓		If they fundamentally alter what people do, training may be necessary. Look at Activities 18–22 to find out more about job skills and at Activities 11–17 to generate more information about capabilities before making a final decision.
Does the change/action imply new or revised knowledge and skills?	✓		Define the knowledge and skills required. Look at Activities 11—22 to compare the new expectations with what people do now before making a final decision.
Does the change/action imply demand for more people?	✓		Find out at what levels. Look at Activities 11–22 to find out the potential already available.
Does the change/action imply recruitment of new people to the organization?	✓		Find out at what levels. Check that appropriate orientation and departmental training is available.
Are the perceptions accurate?	✓	✓	Find out what the people at the top of the organization are prepared to do. Define the inaccuracy and investigate how it has happened.

Questions	Y	N	Responses
Is this information telling us something that we did not know?	✓		Define what has come to light. Describe the implications on the way the organization is run.
		✓	Now that perceptions have been confirmed, find out what the people at the top are prepared to do about this.
Is it important that we change what we do?	✓		Note the changes that will have the biggest impact on perceptions. Describe them in behavioral terms if appropriate, e.g., what people will have to do differently.
		✓	With the help of the people at the top of the organization, work out why it is not important and prepare feedback about this.
Can we change what we do?	✓		Find out who will have to make changes and in what way. Look at Activities 11–17 to see what people do now before making a final decision.
		✓	Investigate the barriers to change. Help those concerned to develop strategies for overcoming the barriers. Highlight the consequences of not changing.
Does this indicate that our employees will be willing to implement the changes we have already planned, in order to further develop the organization?	✓		
		✓	Proceed with action plans. Identify the barriers and ways of overcoming or minimizing them. Look at Activities 18–22 for further information before deciding what to do.

How to Identify Training Needs

From the above descriptions you will realize that there will be some occasions when the information requires further analysis before training needs become apparent (generally discussed in sections (A) and (B)). At other times, you will be working with information that has immediately identified an apparent training need. Sections (C) and (D) generally fall into this category.

The activities in sections (A) and (B) are acting as catalysts for finding out more information. To turn the proposed changes for developing the organization's training needs, use the following checklist of questions and responses for each of the changes and actions.

1st part of checklist

Sometimes the answers to these questions will be *No,* or the impact on people will be minimal. Not all changes and actions will generate training needs. There will be other means of conveying what is happening, by organizational communication for example. It might be worth looking at Activity 6 (see p. 57) in section (B) to make sure that communications are working successfully. This is an effective way of using the activities in section (B) to support other actions, because they give a clear indication of what is happening to people.

When using the section (B) "Organizational Climate" activities on their own, the following checklist of questions and responses will be helpful. This time a negative response might still indicate a training need.

2nd part of checklist

It is important to repeat some of the activities in section (B) from time to time as a means of measuring progress made on achieving change and positively altering the climate of the organization.

Training Strategies

Your next step is to work out how best to implement your training needs. You have several options to consider. The most widely used strategies are described for you on the following page, together with their benefits and potential problems.

Your choice of training strategy may also reveal some additional training needs. For example, if you decide that on-the-job coaching is the best method, then make sure there is someone available with the necessary job and coaching skills. Remember, you will not always be the direct trainer. You will have to take these issues into account as you bring together all of the information generated, the training needs, and your selection of training strategies into a training plan.

Training Plans

At this stage you must first review your objectives and decide if you have achieved what you set out to do; second, think about the expectations of the people involved, such as your sponsor, the respondents to the activities, other managers; and third, decide how best to present your findings and proposed training plans.

Option	Benefits	Potential problems
On-the-job training	• learning in the workplace • provides an example and standard to copy • useful for job skills training • low cost	• interruptions in the workplace • trainer capability • bad habits perpetuated
On-the-job coaching	• learning in the workplace • individuals solve their own problems • meets individual needs • useful for management skills development • low cost	• interruptions in the workplace • recognizing suitable opportunities • capabilities of the coach
Off-the-job Training Courses	• groups exchange ideas • useful for job skills training and management development • safe environment to make mistakes	• disruption to workplace • unreal environment • can be costly
Special projects	• learning in the workplace • combines with on-the-job coaching • opportunities for development clearly identified • low cost	• capabilities of the coach • fitting into existing teams • authority and responsibility must be clearly defined
Open learning	• learning at own pace • supports other methods • brings everyone to the same level of knowledge	• requires high level of self-motivation • can be costly

There are three options:

1. Write a report, circulate it, and ask for comments about the content.
2. Make a presentation and support it with a report.
3. Hold individual meetings to present the proposals.

Ask yourself these questions to help you make an appropriate choice. Use the space for notes to record your own ideas.

Questions	*Notes*

• What did I say I would do at the start?
 	
• What is the communicative style here?
 	
   – Do people usually read reports?
   – Are they used to attending presentations?
   – How much time do they have for individual meetings?
   – Will the same format suit everyone?
 	
• Who must be involved:
 	
   – to give approval?
   – to give support?
 	
• Does everyone require the same amount of information?
 	
• How can I best monitor the proposed training plans?	

You will probably choose to produce a written document of some kind to illustrate your findings. Think about the various activities that you can incorporate into your final presentation. From section (A), "Developing the Organization," there will be action plans and analysis summaries to include in a report (see Activities 2 and 5 for examples of these). From section (B), "Organizational Climate," there will be consolidated findings to present (see examples in Activities 7 and 8). From section (C), "Managing Resources," there will be action plans and consolidated findings that will be useful in your presentations. Activity 12 combines both of these in one comprehensive document. From section (D), "Job Skills," many of the forms within the activities can be used as the basis for training records and plans. For example, the task competencies chart in Activity 20 provides the department's manager with training requirements, probably saving you the time and effort of producing any further exercises.

It is important to make your communication clear and concise. The format below might be useful for your reports:

Content

Summary

Introduction

Methodology

Analysis of data

Conclusions

Recommendations

Appendices

Following are some examples of formats you might use to present your information. (See Tables C, D, and E.)

The first chart shows how one training manager has summarized training that has already taken place. This could be used to review training throughout the organization, by department, or by job.

Name	Department	Training Received	Training Strategy
J. Clay	Marketing	Responsibility at work	External off-the-job course
H. Wood	Stock control	Telephone sales	In-house off-the-job course
M. Tinney	Personnel	Job instruction Communication skills	External off-the-job courses

The next chart shows how another trainer recorded training needs. This chart enables the trainer to identify training requirements that are common to more than one category of employee in the same department. It can be adapted to show areas of common training needs throughout an organization.

POSITION	TRAINING REQUIREMENT
Marketing manager Buyers Buyers' assistants Secretaries	Communications: 1. The importance of communications 2. Effective use of the telephone 3. Effective use of the fax
Buyers	Effective negotiation techniques
Buyers Buyers' assistants	Effective short- and long-range planning

The final chart shows a straightforward way of presenting detailed training plans for departments and individuals.

Name/position	Training objective	Method	Cost	Time frame	Success indicators
Stock control manager Stock controller	To be able to use effective managerial and supervisory skills in the day-to-day running of the stock control and commodities section.	Internal off-the-job course On-the-job coaching	$150 $0	Begin in next 3 months	1. Performance of team members 2. Relations with team members 3. Quality of output from sections

Name/position	Training objective	Method	Cost	Time frame	Success indicators
K. Hughes	To use production planning and line balancing techniques in the day-to-day control of production output.	External off-the-job training course	$750	Before August	1. Daily production figures 2. Effective time balancing 3. Standards improved by 10%

These are thorough training plans based on training objectives that clearly show what the training is intended to achieve together with indicators of success. Showing the cost of this training makes it easier to decide whether the benefits to be gained justify the investment.

It is worthwhile spending time making sure that your process of identifying and presenting the training needs reflects an accurate picture of what is happening in the organization. This will enable you and others to make decisions founded on fact that will have an impact on all those who have been involved in using the activities.

Table A. Starting Your Analysis

Who is my sponsor/champion?	Who are the likely target group(s)?	Which activities will achieve this?	What do I want to find out?	What are the triggers? Are there links?

Table B. Activity Log

Activity	Target group	Number of people involved	Response rate	Quality of information generated

Table C. Training Record

Name	Department	Training received	Training strategy

Table D. Training Needs

Position	Training requirement

Table E. Training Plan

Name/position	Training objective	Method	Cost	Time frame	Success indicators

PART TWO

The Activities

A

Developing the Organization

This section explores potential developments as seen by the people at the top. It contains five activities:

1. Focus on Perceptions
2. Measures of Success
3. Organizational Profile
4. Defining Excellence
5. Customer Satisfaction

The target group are the decision makers in the organization and, by their nature, these activities generate confidential information that will require careful planning by those involved to ensure it is used effectively.

"Focus on Perceptions" reviews what the organization is good at, the aspects of the organization that could be improved, the opportunities the organization has to develop, and the potential hazards it must take action to avoid.

"Measures of Success" sets targets for future organizational development and the steps to take to achieve it.

"Organizational Profile" shows how the performance of the organization is perceived by its top managers. A comparison of the different views will generate a wide range of material for discussion and action.

"Defining Excellence" specifies what the organization has to do to be the best in its marketplace or arena.

"Customer Satisfaction" asks customers to rate the organization's performance in meeting their needs. It will highlight areas of strength to build on and aspects that could cause problems if not addressed.

Developing the organization will not be a part of the role of every trainer, so first ask yourself: "Is this my job?" If your answer is *No*, move on to the next section. If your answer is *Yes*, check that you have made adequate preparations to ensure success on this aspect of training needs analysis. Using the following checklist to prepare.

Preparation	Y	N	Action
Have you: 1. Identified and won the support of a sponsor from the top of the organization? 2. Clarified your objectives — do you know what you want to achieve from using the activity? 3. Assessed the potential problems of using the activities in this organization and made contingencies for them? 4. Selected the most appropriate method for collecting the information from the options given in the activity? 5. Prepared your presentation for the target group?			

1

Focus on Perceptions

Objectives

- To generate information about current organizational performance and the potential impact of internal and external factors on future performance.
- To highlight the perceptions of different individuals about these issues.

Description

This activity is based on a grid which uses statements to generate ideas.

Materials

1. Sufficient copies of Exercise 1.1.
2. A meeting room.

Collecting Information

Methods	Benefits	Potential problems
Grid completed individually.	• Easy to administer. • All points of view brought out.	• Large amount of information to be exchanged. • Harder to achieve consensus.
Group discussion.	• Consensus of opinion is easier to reach. • Takes less time. • Involves everyone immediately.	• Some points of view could be lost. • Dominant views take over.

Methods

A. Grid completed individually.
1. Explain the purpose of the activity to the target group.
2. Give a copy of Exercise 1.1 to each person and agree to a time limit for completion.
3. Hold a meeting with the target group, allowing at least two hours.
4. Ask each person to present their completed grid.
5. Lead a group discussion to achieve a consensus about the perceptions highlighted by the grid. Create a plan for action.

B. Group discussion.
1. Explain the purpose of the activity to the target group.
2. Hold a meeting with the group, allowing at least two hours.
3. Together, brainstorm all issues and factors.
4. Prioritize these onto Exercise 1.1, and ensure that each person receives a copy.
5. Create a plan for action that has the support of the entire group.

Exercise 1.1: Focus on Perceptions

Our organization is good at:	Our organization is let down by:
Internal and external factors in the future that will provide opportunities for our organization to develop are:	Internal and external factors that could pose a threat to our organization in the future are:

Action Plan
What must we do to tip the balance in our favor?

2

Measures of Success

Objectives

- To generate information about the future goals of the organization.
- To plan how these goals will be achieved.

Description

This activity uses a card sort approach to prioritize measures of success. The information then forms the basis of an action plan that shows the steps required to achieve success.

Materials

1. Sufficient copies of Exercise 2.1 cut up and pasted onto cards and organized into packs. Use 3 × 5 cards cut in half. (You can also paste the sheet on cardboard and cut.)
2. Sufficient copies of Exercise 2.2.
3. A meeting room.
4. Flipchart and pens.

Collecting Information

Methods	Benefits	Potential problems
One-on-one interviews.	• All points of view will be heard. • Easily arranged with individuals.	Time-consuming.
Group work.	• Takes less time. • Builds on group commitment immediately.	• Problems of getting people together. • Points of view may be lost.

Methods

A. One-to-one interviews.

1. Brief the target group on the purpose of the activity.
2. Arrange an interview with each person, allowing approximately one hour per interview.
3. Ask each person to sort the cards (Exercise 2.1) by putting the measures of success into priority order.
4. Ask each person to state an achievable percentage target for the most important measures of success.
5. Produce a report that shows the measures of success most often selected as high priority together with their target percentages.
6. Arrange a meeting with the target group, allowing at least two hours.
7. Present the report and lead a discussion to agree on the priorities and the steps for action.
8. Summarize the steps for action onto the plan (Exercise 2.2) and ensure that each person receives a copy.

B. Group work.

1. Brief the target group on the purpose of the activity.
2. Hold a meeting with the group, allowing at least two hours.
3. Organize subgroups to sort the cards (Exercise 2.1) into priority order and to set achievable percentage targets.
4. Ask each subgroup to present its findings.
5. Lead a discussion to agree on the priority measures of success and the steps to be put in place to achieve them.
6. Summarize the steps onto the action plan (Exercise 2.2) and ensure that each person receives a copy.

Exercise 2.1: Measures of Success

We have reduced customer waiting time by X%	We have improved product reliability by X%	We have increased our domestic market share by X%	We have provided all employees with X days' training	We have reduced materials wastage by X%
We have reduced customer complaints by X%	We have increased investment in R&D by X%	We have increased our client base by X%	We have reduced labor turnover by X%	We have reduced outstanding debts from customers by X%
We have improved product availability by X%	We have reduced product manufacture time by X%	We have sold our products to X new countries	We have improved punctuality and attendance by X%	We have improved our unit cost by X%
We respond to all customer inquiries within X hours	We have extended our product range by X%	We have increased our product price by X%	We have carried out performance appraisals with all employees	We have reduced distribution costs by X%
We have increased the level of repeat business to X%	We have imported the reliability of delivery times of our suppliers by X%	We have expanded our business into X new market sectors	We have increased savings from implementing employees' suggestions by X%	We have improved our gross profit by X%

Reproduced from *Training Needs Analysis Toolkit,* Sharon Bartram and
Brenda Gibson, Gower, Aldershot, 1995

Exercise 2.2: Action Plan

Time frame						
Steps to be taken						
Measure of success						

35

3

Organizational Profile

Objectives

- To generate information about the current performance of the organization.
- To identify areas for action to improve efficiency and to achieve the goals of the organization.

Description

This activity is based on a series of open-ended statements about particular aspects of an organization to which people respond.

Materials

1. Sufficient copies of Exercise 3.1.
2. Meeting room.

Collecting Information

Methods	Benefits	Potential problems
Survey for self-completion.	• Takes less time. • Easy to administer.	Ideas are not probed.
One-on-one interviews.	• Allows ideas to be probed.	Time-consuming.
Group discussion.	• Ideas are shared. • Less time-consuming.	• Dominant views prevail. • Finding an opportunity to bring people together.

Methods

A. Survey for self-completion.
1. Explain the purpose of the activity to the target group.
2. Give a copy of Exercise 3.1 to each person and agree to a time limit for completion.
3. Collect the surveys and analyze by identifying similarities and differences in the responses.
4. Prepare a report that clarifies the areas for action.
5. Arrange a meeting of the target group to present the findings and to gain agreement to an action plan.

B. One-on-one interviews.
1. Explain the purpose of the activity to the target group.
2. Arrange interviews with each person, allowing approximately one hour per interview.
3. Use the statements in Exercise 3.1 as the basis for each discussion.
4. Probe the responses to clarify meaning.
5. Record the responses on Exercise 3.1.
6. Prepare a report on the outcomes of the interviews that highlights the areas for action.
7. Arrange a meeting of the target group to present the findings and gain agreement to an action plan.

C. Group discussion.
1. Explain the purpose of the activity to the target group.
2. Arrange a meeting to discuss the issues, allowing approximately two hours.
3. Use the statements in Exercise 3.1 as a basis for the discussion and probe responses to clarify meaning.
4. Summarize the discussion by stating the areas for action that will have emerged and gain agreement to an action plan.

Exercise 3.1: Organizational Profile

This survey is designed to help you to think about your organization as it is at the present time.

Complete the following statements, giving as much detail as you can. Your information will provide the basis for deciding future actions.

Service

1. In describing our overall level of service, I would say:

2. Our customers would describe our service to them as:

3. When dealing with queries, customers would say we are:

4. In responding to customers' specific needs, our systems are:

5. Customers would say our reliability is:

39

Reproduced from *Training Needs Analysis Toolkit,* Sharon Bartram and
Brenda Gibson, Gower, Aldershot, 1995

? *Exercise 3.1 (continued)*

Products

6. In describing the quality of our products, I would say:

7. In describing the effectiveness of our products, I would say:

8. This organization's attitude toward research and development is:

9. In describing the appropriateness of the technologies used to produce our products, I would say:

10. In describing the systems we have of ensuring consistency of quality, I would say:

40

Marketplace

11. The organization's position in the marketplace is:

12. When asked who our customers are, I would say:

13. When asked who our competitors are, I would say:

14. Our customers choose our products because:

15. The untapped markets for our products are:

People

16. The organization's attitude toward its people is:

and is reflected by:

41

Reproduced from *Training Needs Analysis Toolkit,* Sharon Bartram and
Brenda Gibson, Gower, Aldershot, 1995

? *Exercise 3.1 (continued)*

17. The qualities in people that we reward are:

18. In describing communication in this organization, I would say:

19. The standards to which this organization trains its people are:

20. Employees' attitudes toward this organization are reflected by:

21. The main reasons for labor turnover in this organization are:

22. In describing the levels of absenteeism and sick leave in this organization, I would say:

Reproduced from *Training Needs Analysis Toolkit,* Sharon Bartram and
Brenda Gibson, Gower, Aldershot, 1995

23. This organization identifies people with potential by:

24. If a person in a key position left unexpectedly tomorrow, this organization would fill the gap by:

25. In describing this organization's methods of recruitment and selection, I would say:

Control

26. Financially this organization is:

27. When comparing our costs to budgets, I would say:

Reproduced from *Training Needs Analysis Toolkit,* Sharon Bartram and Brenda Gibson, Gower, Aldershot, 1995

? *Exercise 3.1 (concluded)*

28. When describing the adequacy of our systems of monitoring costs, I would say:

29. The steps we take to improve cash flow are:

30. The aspects of the organization where we apply most control are:

In summing up the description of our organization, the main points I would make are:

4

Defining Excellence

Objectives

- To assess the performance of the organization against similar organizations and/or competitors.
- To generate information that defines excellence within the context of the organization and its capabilities.
- To identify how this excellence will be achieved.

Description

This activity uses a grid to record the information generated.

Materials

1. Sufficient copies of Exercise 4.1.
2. A meeting room.
3. Flipchart and pens.

Collecting Information

Method	Benefits	Potential problems
Group work.	• Shared ideas. • Shared commitment to action.	Getting individuals together.

Method

Group work.
1. Explain the purpose of the activity to the target group and explain the usefulness of researching the activities of other organizations.
2. Carry out preliminary research of similar organizations and/or competitors using libraries, visits, and so on to gather information.
3. Produce a report on the findings and circulate this to the target group.

4. Hold a meeting to discuss the findings and to define standards of excellence for the organization. Allow at least two hours for this.
5. Give a copy of Exercise 4.1 to each person and check for understanding.
6. Brainstorm to define the standards of excellence for each area on the grid.
7. Lead a discussion to identify the actions necessary to achieve the standards and ask each person to record these details on the grid.
8. Assist the group in agreeing on the priority areas and deciding on their first actions.

Exercise 4.1: Defining Excellence

Standards of excellence	The facilities and equipment we require are:	The skills our employees require are:	The skills our managers require are:	The structures and systems we require are:
Service:				
Product:				
Market:				
People:				
Control:				

5

Customer Satisfaction

Objectives

- To generate information about customer needs and their level of satisfaction with the organization.
- To identify areas for action to meet more effectively the needs of customers.

Description

This activity is a survey that combines two elements: selecting aspects of the organization's product or service that are important and rating the organization's performance in these aspects.

Materials

1. Sufficient copies of Exercise 5.1.
2. Exercise 5.2 for completion.
3. A meeting room.

Collecting Information

Methods	Benefits	Potential problems
Mailed survey.	• Increased sample size. • Ease of administration.	• Low return.
One-on-one interviews.	• Opportunity to probe information. • Guarantees response level.	• Time needed. • Smaller sample size.

Methods

A. Mailed survey.

1. Select a sample of customers and inform them about the purpose of the activity.
2. Send each customer a copy of Exercise 5.1 indicating the time frame for return.
3. Analyze the replies, using Exercise 5.2 to record the findings.
4. Communicate the findings by written report to the target group.
5. Hold a meeting with the target group to discuss the findings and identify steps for action. Allow at least one hour.

B. One-on-one interviews.

1. Select a sample of customers and inform them about the purpose of the activity.
2. Arrange and carry out interviews with each customer, using Exercise 5.1 as the basis for the discussion. Allow at least one hour per interview.
3. Analyze the information from each interview, using Exercise 5.2 to summarize the findings.
4. Communicate the findings by written report to the target group.
5. Hold a meeting with the target group to discuss the findings and identify steps for action. Allow at least one hour.

Exercise 5.1: Customer Satisfaction

As an organization we value you as a customer and in order to meet your expectations of us we would appreciate your cooperation in completing this survey. The information you provide will help us to assess how best to provide a level of service that keeps you returning to us time after time. These details will, of course, be treated in the strictest confidence.

The survey comprises two stages: first, read the list of items and select (indicate with a checkmark ✓) those which are important to you when dealing with our organization; second, rate (indicate with a checkmark ✓) your satisfaction with our performance against these items. The categories are defined as: HS, highly satisfied; S, satisfied; D, dissatisfied; and HD, highly dissatisfied.

We look forward to reviewing your responses and we may ask you to participate again as a way of monitoring our progress. We hope we can count on your continued assistance.

Thank you.

	Item	Level of satisfaction			
		HS	S	D	HD
	Quality				
	Design				
	Delivery speed				
	Price				
	Knowledgeable staff				
	After-sales service				
	Receiving information frequently				
	Delivery reliability				
	Performance				
	Product range				
	Receiving information about innovations				
	Seeing the right people				
	Locality				
	Reliability				
	Value for money				
	Flexible systems to respond to needs				
	Manner of the contact staff				
	Features and options				
	Response time				
	Things are right first time				
	Other (please specify)				

Reproduced from *Training Needs Analysis Toolkit*, Sharon Bartram and Brenda Gibson, Gower, Aldershot, 1995

Exercise 5.2: Customer Satisfaction Analysis

Item	Times chosen	Total HS	Total S	Total D	Total HD
Quality					
Design					
Delivery speed					
Price					
Knowledgeable staff					
After-sales service					
Receiving information frequently					
Delivery reliability					
Performance					
Product range					
Receiving information about innovations					
Seeing the right people					
Locality					
Reliability					
Value for money					
Flexible systems to respond to needs					
Manner of the contact staff					
Features and options					
Response time					
Things are right first time					
Other (please specify)					

B

Organizational Climate

This section measures employees' perceptions of the organization and raises these issues for debate with the people at the top, who must make a commitment to change before the activities are used. The way an organization is perceived by its employees is an important indicator of how people outside might also see it and is one which could affect its long-term success. There are five activities in this section:

6. Communications
7. Work Fulfillment
8. What Drives This Organization?
9. Evidence of Equality
10. Is This a Learning Organization?

The target group are all the organization's employees, but the initiative for this work must come from the top. It would be reckless to use these activities without that support, as they will raise people's consciousness about what is going on around them and so awaken expectations. To do this and then fail to react would have an adverse impact on the organization from which it could take a long time to recover.

"Communications" reflects people's views on the improvements the organization could make.

"Work Fulfillment" highlights the levels of job satisfaction within the organization along with attitudes toward authority, work planning, communications, and work methods.

"What Drives This Organization?" shows whether the managers at the top are consistently conveying the values of the organization to the work force.

"Evidence of Equality" researches the organization's achievements in providing equality of opportunity in all aspects. It shows where equal treatment exists and where there have been instances of direct or indirect discrimination.

"Is This a Learning Organization?" examines employees' perceptions of how the organization treats them and their futures.

Organizational climate may not be a part of the role of every trainer, so first ask yourself "Is this my job?" If your answer is *No,* move on to the next section. If your answer is *Yes,* check that you have made the preparations that are necessary to the success of this aspect of training needs analysis. Use the following checklist as your guide.

Preparation	Y	N	Action
Have you 1. Identified and won the support of the appropriate sponsor?			
2. Clarified your objectives — do you know what you want to achieve from using the activity?			
3. Assessed the potential problems of using the activities in this organization and made contingencies for them?			
4. Assessed the potential problems of using the activities with this target group and made contingencies for them?			
5. Considered the expectations taking part will raise, and discussed them with your sponsor and other managers?			
6. Selected the best method of collecting the information from the options given in the activity?			
7. Prepared your presentation for the target group?			

6

Communications

Objectives

- To generate information about how communication in the organization is perceived.
- To collect ideas from employees on how communication could be improved.
- To identify areas of the organization that will help or hinder the achievement of these improvements.

Description

This activity uses brainstorming techniques to provide a quantity of ideas that are then evaluated for priority order and analyzed.

Materials

1. Sufficient copies of Exercise 6.1.
2. Prepared flipcharts (See Trainer's Notes A).
3. Copy of Trainer's Notes B for reference.
4. Meeting room.
5. Flipchart paper, pens and adhesive-backed stars or other shapes (available from office stationers).

Collecting Information

Methods	Benefits	Potential problems
Group discussions: • all employees at each level • sample of employees at each level • mixture of levels across a function/department.	• Generates solutions. • Highly participative. • A safe way to express opinions.	• Time needed to assemble groups and complete the activity. • Solutions could be contrary to current management styles.

Methods	Benefits	Potential problems
Group discussions to establish priorities followed by a meeting with management to identify changes.	• Easy to administer. • Involves decision makers earlier in the process.	Employees not involved in identifying changes so could limit commitment.

Methods

A. Group discussion for entire process.
1. Explain the purpose of the activity to the target group.
2. Arrange meetings with groups of between 10 and 15 people, allowing one hour per meeting.
3. During each meeting distribute Exercise 6.1 and explain the brainstorming technique. You might find a warm-up topic useful, such as "Uses for a ball of string." This ensures understanding of the technique and helps to remove inhibitions.
4. Using your prepared flipchart A (see Trainer's Notes A) begin the brainstorming, maintaining the momentum until the group runs out of ideas.
5. Evaluate the brainstorm list by removing duplicated ideas and asking the group for links between ideas. Write the consolidated list onto a new flipchart.
6. Give each group member 10 adhesive stars, which they are to share among the listed ideas for improvements to identify the priorities as they see them. They can give more than one star to one idea. If they see one improvement as more important than any other, they could allocate all ten stars to it.
7. Add up the total number of stars given to each improvement idea and underline the top five with the highest scores. Ask the group to enter them onto Exercise 6.1.
8. Using your prepared flipcharts B, C, and D (see Trainer's Notes A), ask for contributions relating to each heading. The questions on Trainer's Notes B are suggested prompts for this discussion.
9. Close the meeting by explaining that the information generated by each group will be consolidated into a report about which they will receive feedback.
10. Produce a report showing the trends in suggested improvements and the improvements that are seen as priorities. Summarize the report with the changes to make, benefits to be realized, and potential problems to be overcome to achieve the improvements.
11. Distribute and discuss the findings with senior managers/ decision makers and agree on actions to be taken.
12. Give feedback to the target group.

B. Group discussions to establish priorities followed by a meeting with management to identify changes.
Follow steps 1 to 7 and conclude the group meetings at this point.

8. Arrange meetings with managers to assess the priority improvements suggested by the groups. Use your prepared flipcharts B, C, and D (see Trainer's Notes) as a framework for discussion.
9. Agree on actions for implementing the improvements.
10. Produce a report that summarizes the outcomes and feedback for the target group.

Exercise 6.1: Communications

Brainstorming

Brainstorming is a technique designed to generate a number of ideas about a particular topic. Contribute your ideas freely, whatever they are, because the more ideas that are generated, the more likely you are to find quality solutions to the issues.

Rules of brainstorming:

- Do not be critical of any idea.
- Defer any judgments about ideas.
- Quantity of ideas is all important.
- Building on ideas is useful.
- Allow freewheeling thought and wild ideas.

Record the priority ideas from your group's brainstorming exercise:

"Improving Communications"

Top priority: _____

_____

_____

_____

_____

Trainer's Notes A: Communications

Prepare your flipcharts as shown below:

A

> Ways of improving
> communications in
> the organization

B	C	D
What changes would you make to achieve the priority improvements?	What benefits are to be gained from the priority improvements?	What potential problems must be overcome in order to achieve the priority improvements?

Trainer's Notes B: Communications

Suggested Questions

- How is news and information from the top organization usually disseminated?

- How do we use indirect methods of communication, such as bulletin boards and newsletters, to spread news and information?

- What opportunities are there for expression of ideas?

- How effective are we at communicating the message to the right people at the right time?

- Is there a grapevine working here?

- What feedback do you receive if, for example, you offer a suggestion for improvement?

- How are you encouraged to have ideas and to express your views?

- Is communication on a "need to know" basis only?

- How regularly do we communicate here?

- What types of communication do we use here –

  — telling you what to do?
  — giving you details of results and future plans?
  — consulting you for your views?
  — involving you in decisions?

Reproduced from *Training Needs Analysis Toolkit,* Sharon Bartram and
Brenda Gibson, Gower, Aldershot, 1995

7

Work Fulfillment

Objective

- To generate information about levels of job satisfaction and attitudes toward the way authority, work-planning, communications, and work methods operate at departmental and organizational levels.

Description

This activity is a survey that requires employees to consider twenty paired statements in relation to their work situation. By comparing the statements and placing a mark on a scale, employees can describe their situation as they see it.

Materials

1. Sufficient copies of Exercises 7.1 and 7.2.
2. Copy of Exercise 7.3.
3. A meeting room.

Collecting Information

Methods	Benefits	Potential problems
Mailed survey.	• Easy to administer. • Generates information quickly.	• Poor response rate. • Worries about confidentiality.
Survey completed individually followed by individual meetings.	• Able to check understanding. • Reassure about confidentiality.	Time-consuming.

67

Methods	Benefits	Potential problems
Survey completed individually followed by group meetings.	• Able to check understanding. • Reassure about confidentiality. • Explore common ground.	• Disruptive to workplace. • Minority views overlooked.
Survey used as basis for individual discussion.	Encourages disclosure.	• Time-consuming.
Survey used as basis for group discussion.	Speeds up gathering of information.	• Stifles disclosure. • Dominant views suppress others.

Methods

A. Mailed survey.
1. Decide whether to collect information on a departmental basis (Exercise 7.1) or on an organizational basis (Exercise 7.2).
2. Explain the purpose of the activity to the target group, stressing that there will be feedback on the findings and agreed upon actions.
3. Distribute a copy of the appropriate survey (either 7.1 or 7.2) to each person and agree on a time limit for completion and return.
4. Analyze the completed surveys using Exercise 7.3. Present the findings to senior managers for discussion and to agree on actions.

B. Survey completed individually followed by individual meetings.
Follow steps 1 and 2 above.

3. Distribute a copy of the appropriate survey, Exercise 7.1 or 7.2, to each person and arrange a follow-up meeting. Allow up to 45 minutes per meeting.
4. During the meeting review the person's completed survey, asking them to explain the reasons for their ratings and to give suggestions for improvements. Note comments made.
5. Take a copy of the completed survey before closing the meeting.
6. When all meetings are complete, analyze the surveys and additional comments using Exercise 7.3.

C. Survey completed individually followed by group meetings.
Follow the six steps described above, organizing group meetings of not more than 12 people and allowing up to one and a half hours per meeting.

D. Survey used as basis for individual discussion.
Follow steps 1 and 2 above.

3. Arrange a meeting with each person, allowing one hour per meeting.
4. During the meetings present the survey, either Exercise 7.1 or 7.2, to the person and ask them to respond. Ask them to explain the reasons for their ratings and to give suggestions for improvements. Write down comments made.

Follow steps 5 and 6 above.

E. Survey used as basis for group discussion.
Follow steps 1 and 2 above.

3. Arrange a series of group meetings with not more than 12 people and allow up to one and a half hours per meeting.
4. During the meetings distribute the survey, Exercise 7.1 or 7.2, to each person. Ask them to respond and explore the reasons behind their ratings and suggestions for improvements. Write down comments made.
5. When all the meetings have taken place, analyze the range of responses to the survey and additional comments, using Exercise 7.3. Present your findings to senior managers for discussion and to agree on actions.

Exercise 7.1: Work Fulfillment

Thinking about your department, read the following paired statements and put a checkmark (✓) at the point on the scale that corresponds most closely to the situation as you see it.

1   2   3   4   5   6

1. I am made fully aware of my achievements and given advice on how to improve my performance.

   I am not given the opportunity to raise the difficulties of my job and I am not informed sufficiently about my performance.

2. Decision making is carried out by consultation with the entire department.

   Decision making involves only the few people in authority within the department.

3. My job is clearly defined and I understand what I am expected to do.

   My job overlaps with others so that I am not clear about what I have to do.

4. Work is planned so that time schedules can be met.

   Work planning is haphazard, leading to difficulties meeting time schedules.

5. Objectives are clearly defined for my section.

   I do not have a clear idea of the aims and objectives of my section.

6. I have a clear understanding of the aims of the other sections within the department.

   No one quite knows what other people are doing.

7. There is a well-defined system of line management, therefore, I know whom to go to with my problems.

   Line management is not well defined, therefore, I am not clear whom to go to with my problems.

8. I feel I am encouraged to develop my potential and that I am making progress.

   I feel I am not encouraged to develop my potential and consequently I am not making progress.

71

		1	2	3	4	5	6	

9. The different sections within the department work well together achieving a high standard of effectiveness. | There is considerable friction and lack of co-operation between different sections in the department not achieving a high standard of effectiveness.

10. I am able to use my own initiative to achieve results when tackling the duties of my job. | I work within the constraints of predetermined procedures to achieve results.

11. There is OPEN communication — motives, objectives, and plans are discussed openly. | There is CLOSED communication — motives, objectives, and plans are hidden.

12. The search for improved working methods is encouraged and my ideas are heard. | We just continue in the same old way with no change in working methods.

13. There is commitment from my section to the work at hand with everyone's knowledge and skills being used to create a team identity. | Individuals in my section are left to their own devices with their knowledge and skills not being used to the fullest.

14. I seldom have time to wonder what to do next. | Work planning lacks organization so that I find I have slack periods throughout the day.

15. Work relationships are designed in such a way that I feel I am able to make a positive contribution to the department because my voice will be heard. | Work relationships are designed so that instruction is given and no questions are expected. I feel inhibited by this approach.

16. Individual developmental needs are understood and taken into account. | Individual development needs are handled on a "hit or miss" basis.

Reproduced from *Training Needs Analysis Toolkit*, Sharon Bartram and
Brenda Gibson, Gower, Aldershot, 1995

	1	2	3	4	5	6

17. I feel stimulated by what I am doing and achieving.

I feel discouraged and frustrated by lack of achievement.

18. We work hard because we have a common sense of purpose and not because we are driven.

We are guided more by pressure from above than a sense of commitment.

19. Staff are very flexible and movement between sections is the norm.

Sections tend to operate in a vacuum.

20. The department accepts that conflicts sometimes arise and attempts to find solutions that have the majority's agreement and understanding.

The department does not accept that conflicts arise and leaves problems unresolved, hoping they will disappear.

73

Reproduced from *Training Needs Analysis Toolkit,* Sharon Bartram and Brenda Gibson, Gower, Aldershot, 1995

Exercise 7.2: Work Fulfillment

Thinking about your organization, read the following paired statements and put a checkmark (✓) at the point on the scale that corresponds most closely to the situation as you see it.

	1 2 3 4 5 6	
1.	I am made fully aware of my achievements and given advice on how to improve my performance.	I am not given the opportunity to raise the difficulties of my job and I am not informed sufficiently about my performance.
2.	Decision making is carried out by consultation throughout this organization.	Decision making involves only the few people in authority in this organization.
3.	My job is clearly defined and I understand what I am expected to do.	My job overlaps with others so that I am not clear about what I have to do.
4.	Work is planned so that time schedules can be met.	Work planning is haphazard, leading to difficulties meeting time schedules.
5.	Organizational objectives are clearly defined.	I do not have a clear idea of the aims and objectives of this organization.
6.	I have a clear understanding of the aims of the other departments within the organization.	No one quite knows what other people are doing.
7.	There is a well-defined system of line management, therefore, I know whom to go to with my problems	Line management is not well defined, therefore, I am not clear whom to go to with my problems
8.	I feel I am encouraged to develop my potential and that I am making progress.	I feel I am not encouraged to develop my potential and consequently I am not making progress.

75

Reproduced from *Training Needs Analysis Toolkit,* Sharon Bartram and Brenda Gibson, Gower, Aldershot, 1995

? *Exercise 7.2 (continued)*

| | 1 | 2 | 3 | 4 | 5 | 6 |

9. I am made fully aware of my achievements and given advice on how to improve my performance.

There is considerable friction and lack of co-operation between different departments in the organization not achieving a high standard of effectiveness.

10. I am able to use my own initiative to achieve results when tackling the duties of my job.

I work within the constraints of predetermined procedures to achieve results.

11. There is OPEN communication — motives, objectives, and plans are discussed openly.

There is CLOSED communication — motives, objectives, and plans are hidden.

12. The search for improved working methods is encouraged and my ideas are heard.

We just continue in the same old way with no change in working methods.

13. There is commitment from my department to the work at hand with everyone's knowledge and skills being used to create a team identity.

Individuals in my department are left to their own devices with their knowledge and skills not being used to the fullest.

14. I seldom have time to wonder what to do next.

Work planning lacks organization so that I find I have slack periods throughout the day.

15. Work relationships are designed in such a way that I feel I am able to make a positive contribution to the organization because my voice will be heard.

Work relationships are designed so that instruction is given and no questions are expected. I feel inhibited by this approach.

16. Individual developmental needs are understood and taken into account.

Individual developmental needs are handled on a "hit or miss" basis.

Reproduced from *Training Needs Analysis Toolkit,* Sharon Bartram and Brenda Gibson, Gower, Aldershot, 1995

	1	2	3	4	5	6	

17. I feel stimulated by what I am doing and achieving.

I feel discouraged and frustrated by lack of achievement.

18. We work hard because we have a common sense of purpose and not because we are driven.

We are guided more by pressure from above than a sense of commitment.

19. Staff are very flexible and movement between departments is the norm.

Departments tend to operate in a vacuum.

20. The organization accepts that conflicts sometimes arise and attempts to find solutions that have the majority's agreement and understanding.

The organization does not accept that conflicts arise and leaves problems unresolved, hoping they will disappear.

77

Reproduced from *Training Needs Analysis Toolkit,* Sharon Bartram and
Brenda Gibson, Gower, Aldershot, 1995

Exercise 7.3: Work Fulfillment

Survey Analysis

Total number of people in the survey: _____

Paired statement number	Number of people choosing a rating of:						Additional comments
	1	2	3	4	5	6	
Job satisfaction 1							
3							
8							
10							
16							
17							
18							
Authority 2							
7							
15							
Work planning 4							
5							
6							
14							
Communications 9							
11							
20							
Work methods 12							
13							
19							
Suggestions for improvements:							

79

Reproduced from *Training Needs Analysis Toolkit*, Sharon Bartram and
Brenda Gibson, Gower, Aldershot, 1995

8

What Drives This Organization?

Objectives

- To compare employees' perceptions of what drives their organization based on how they are managed.
- To compare these perceptions with the views of senior managers.
- To suggest changes to management style in order to communicate a clear, consistent message about what drives the organization.

Description

This activity uses a grid technique to compare driving forces of the organization and to identify the priorities within them.

Materials

1. Sufficient copies of Exercises 8.1 and 8.2.
2. A meeting room.

Collecting Information

Methods	Benefits	Potential problems
Mailed survey to: • all employees • random sample • peer group sample • mixed levels sample.	• Easy to administer. • Generates information quickly.	• Low response rate. • Unable to verify understanding.
Completed individually followed by group discussion with: • all employees • random sample • peer group sample • mixed levels sample.	• Ensures high response rate. • Able to verify understanding.	Time.

Methods

A. Mailed survey.

1. Explain the purpose of the activity to the target group, stressing that feedback will be given about the outcomes.
2. Distribute copies of Exercise 8.1 and agree on a time limit for completion and return.
3. At the same time ask senior managers to complete Exercise 8.1 in preparation for a meeting to discuss findings.
4. Analyze the returned grids using Exercise 8.2. Prepare the findings by using a tally system to write down the number of times the options are given top priority and list the range of scores within each option.
5. Arrange a meeting with senior managers to present the findings and compare them to their own completed grids.
6. This meeting should highlight areas of agreement, discrepancies, and any unclear perceptions of what priorities are driving the organization.
7. Conclude the meeting by agreeing on action plans.

B. Completed individually followed by group discussion.

1. Explain the purpose of the activity to the target group, stressing that feedback will be given about the outcomes.
2. Distribute copies of Exercise 8.1 and agree on times for a series of group discussion meetings. Allow up to 30 minutes per meeting. During the meetings check that each person has completed the grid and give clarification. Collect the completed grids.
3. At the same time ask senior managers to complete Exercise 8.1 in preparation for a meeting to discuss findings.

Follow steps 4 to 7 as above.

Exercise 8.1: What Drives This Organization?

The grid below suggests twelve options. The format of the grid allows you to compare the priority of each option against all the others. Follow these steps:

1. Take the first option from *Across*, STABILITY, and compare it with the different options from *Down*.
2. If you feel that STABILITY has a higher priority in your organization than CUSTOMER, put an "A" in the box. If CUSTOMER has the higher priority, put a "D" in the box.
3. Go along the row, each time deciding whether STABILITY has the higher or lower priority and putting an "A" or "D" in the boxes.
4. Repeat the process for CUSTOMER, going along the row and comparing it with all the other options.
5. Repeat for all the other options across, comparing them with all the options down.
6. When this is complete, add up the total number of "A"s allocated to each option across and put the score in the Total "A"s column. Now look down each column and put the total number of "D"s for each option.
7. Your grid is now complete. You will be able to see what you feel is driving your organization. It will be the option that has scored the most when you add up the A and D totals.

Down

	CUSTOMER	INNOVATION	COMMUNITY	POWER	PROFIT	EXPANSION	PEOPLE	QUALITY	SALES	COSTS	PRODUCT	Total "A"s
STABILITY												
CUSTOMER												
INNOVATION												
COMMUNITY												
POWER												
PROFIT												
EXPANSION												
PEOPLE												
QUALITY												
SALES												
COSTS												
PRODUCT												
Total "D"s												

(Across)

Exercise 8.2: What Drives This Organization?

Priority Grid Summary
Total number of respondents: _____

Option	Number of times identified as top priority
STABILITY	
CUSTOMER	
INNOVATION	
COMMUNITY	
POWER	
PROFIT	
EXPANSION	
PEOPLE	
QUALITY	
SALES	
COSTS	
PRODUCT	

Range within each option:

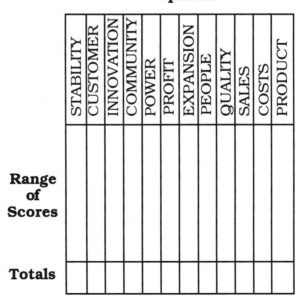

Options

Range of Scores

Totals

85

9

Evidence of Equality

Objectives

- To research the organization's approach to equality.
- To gather evidence indicating positive or negative actions that affect equality within the organization.

Description

This activity is an evidence-gathering exercise on issues relating to equality.

Materials

1. Trainer's Notes A and B for reference.
2. Exercise 9.1.

Collecting Information

Methods	Benefits	Potential problems
Personally gather examples of evidence for analysis and presentation.	Objective information gathered.	Access to information.

Method

Personally gather examples of evidence for analysis and presentation.

1. Plan your approach to gathering evidence. Trainer's Notes A describe the type of evidence relevant to each issue.
2. Gather the information available in your organization.
3. Analyze the evidence you find and categorize into examples of positive and negative actions. Use Trainer's Notes B as your reference and summarize your findings on Exercise 9.1.
4. Arrange a meeting with senior managers to present your findings and agree on actions.

Trainer's Notes A: Evidence of Equality

Issue	Relevant evidence
Promotion	Statistics showing comparisons of who is promoted — male/female; race; age; disability. Organization's written policy on access to training and development. Description of how appraisal is applied with examples of documentation. Records of appraisal training throughout the organization. Content of appraisal training. Examples of notices showing internal vacancies.
Stereotypes	Statistics showing comparisons of who does particular types of work, for example: clerical/managerial; full-time/part-time; manual/technical. Recruitment policy and the criteria used to select people for jobs.
Harassment	Records of complaints made and action taken. Records of interpersonal skills training throughout the organization. Content of interpersonal skills training.
Status	Statistics showing comparisons of who does particular types of work, for example: clerical/managerial; full-time/part-time; manual/technical. Comparison of perks and benefits available between jobs/job grades.
Selection	Recruitment policy and the criteria used to select people for jobs. Examples of job vacancies and the way they are advertised. Records of recruitment training throughout the organization. Content of recruitment training.
Language	Examples of organizational communications, for example: newsletters, reports, and so on. Comparison of job titles. Records of language training made available. Content of language training. Examples of vacancy advertisements.
Work hours	Examples of work rotas. Written terms and conditions.
Pay	Statistical comparisons between male/female; full-time/part-time; different races; age ranges; disabilities.
Leave entitlement	Description of what is available and criteria for access.
Training and development	Training policy and the criteria for access. Comparison of training available to different jobs; job grades; full-time/part-time employees. Examples of methods used to identify training needs. Content of training programs. Range of training methods used: courses; coaching; open learning and so on. Ease of access to training events: venue; times; dates.
Education	Education policy and the criteria for access. Comparison of education available to different employees: male/female; full-time/ part-time; different races; age ranges; disabilities.
Aspirations	Description of how appraisal is applied with examples of documentation. Records of appraisal training. Content of appraisal training. Methods for identifying potential among employees. Criteria for access to opportunities.
Blocks and barriers	Examples of criteria for access to promotion, training, education and so on. Personal experiences of individuals.

Reproduced from *Training Needs Analysis Toolkit,* Sharon Bartram and
Brenda Gibson, Gower, Aldershot, 1995

Trainer's Notes A

Issue	Relevant evidence
Socializing	Examples of networking. Description of organizational events: access; membership, and so on.
Customers' impressions, actual and perceived	Examples of range of customers. Personal experiences of individuals.
Role models	Personal experiences of individuals.
History	Background to the organization. Organizational records.
Influences	Description of location of organization. Background information about the local community. Examples of media influence inside the organization: periodicals; newspapers; radio; television; training materials used; and so on. Art and other visual displays showing positive/negative images of minority groups.
Hierarchies	Organizational charts.

90

Reproduced from *Training Needs Analysis Toolkit,* Sharon Bartram and Brenda Gibson, Gower, Aldershot, 1995

Trainer's Notes B: Evidence of Equality

Testing the Evidence

For each piece of evidence you gather ask yourself these three questions:

1. Does the evidence show equal treatment?

In other words, do all sections of the organization have equal opportunity and access based on their knowledge and skills?

For example: You would know that equal treatment existed if you were called into a meeting and you were unable to predict the make-up of the group who would be present in terms of race, color, sex, sexual orientation, disability, age, and so on.

2. Does the evidence show direct discrimination?

In other words, are people treated less favorably than others on the grounds of race, color, ethnic or national origin, sex, sexual orientation, marital status, disability, or age?

For example: A college used a pre-selection process that automatically ensured that white male candidates were selected for interviews while non-white female candidates were not, regardless of any other criteria.

3. Does the evidence show indirect discrimination?

In other words, are there any rules, requirements, or conditions that are equally applied to all but have a disproportionate adverse impact on some and cannot be justified as reasonable or necessary on employment-related grounds?

For example: A company was recruiting camera technicians and stipulated that candidates must have a degree in physics, even though this was not necessary to perform the job. This requirement had a disproportionately adverse impact on women, who were less likely to have this degree than men.

91

Reproduced from *Training Needs Analysis Toolkit,* Sharon Bartram and
Brenda Gibson, Gower, Aldershot, 1995

Exercise 9.1: Testing the Evidence

Evidence	Describe the ways in which the evidence shows:			Action
	Equal treatment	Direct discrimination	Indirect discrimination	

Reproduced from *Training Needs Analysis Toolkit,* Sharon Bartram and
Brenda Gibson, Gower, Aldershot, 1995

10

Is This a Learning Organization?

Objective

- To generate information about employee's perceptions on the commitment of the organization to training and development.

Description

This activity uses structured discussions to elicit information. Separate discussion exercises are available for people at different levels within the organization.

Materials

1. Sufficient copies of Exercises 10.1 — 10.5.
2. A meeting room.
3. Blank paper.

Collecting Information

Methods	Benefits	Potential problems
Individual interviews with people at different levels of the organization.	• All views taken into account. • Thorough analysis of the situation	• Numbers included. • Time consuming.
Group discussions with peer groups.	Speeds up information gathering.	• Dominant views stifle other contributions. • Time to assemble people.

Methods

A. Individual interviews with people at different levels of the organization.

1. Decide whether to include all employees or a representative sample.
2. Explain the purpose of the activity to the target group.
3. Arrange individual meetings, allowing up to one hour for each.
4. Select the appropriate Exercises from 10.1 — 10.5, according to the level of the individual in the organization. During the meetings use the exercise to encourage comment and to record the information generated.
5. Produce a summary of the information gathered from each level of employee. Circulate the summary to the people involved for their comments and agreement.
6. Produce a report using the key points from each summary to provide information about the whole organization.
7. Discuss this report with senior managers to identify action points.

B. Group discussions with peer groups.

Follow steps 1 and 2 above.

3. Arrange group meetings of not more than 12 people. Allow at least one and a half hours per meeting.

Follow steps 4 to 7 above.

Exercise 10.1: Senior managers/Decision makers

QUESTIONS	KEY POINTS
1. What link do you see between the organization's business plan and training and development?	
2. Is training and development viewed as an investment or a cost?	
3. How is the budget for training and development decided upon?	
4. How much resource is allocated to the budget?	
5. How is the budget usually spent?	
6. How much responsibility do managers have for managing this budget?	
7. What are your expectations of your managers and employees in general?	
8. How do you communicate these expectations to the people concerned?	
9. How do you monitor to see if people achieve your expectations?	
10. What happens when people do achieve your expectations?	

Reproduced from *Training Needs Analysis Toolkit,* Sharon Bartram and
Brenda Gibson, Gower, Aldershot, 1995

? *Exercise 10.1 (concluded)*

QUESTIONS	KEY POINTS
11. What happens when people do not achieve your expectations?	
12. What will the organization look like in five years' time?	
13. What knowledge and skill will be needed: • at your level • at other levels?	
14. Which of these do you already possess: • at your level • at other levels?	
15. Which of these will need to be developed: • at your level • at other levels?	
16. How do you identify potential?	
17. How do you prepare people for change?	
18. What types of learning opportunities do you offer: • external courses • in-house courses • projects • on-the-job coaching?	
19. What are the priorities in training and development for the next twelve months?	
20. Why?	

98

Reproduced from *Training Needs Analysis Toolkit*, Sharon Bartram and Brenda Gibson, Gower, Aldershot, 1995

Exercise 10.2: Managers Managing Other Managers

QUESTIONS	KEY POINTS
1. What link do you see between your departmental objectives and training and development?	
2. Is training and development viewed as an investment or a cost?	
3. How realistic is the budget for training and development?	
4. How much have you spent on training and development in the past twelve months?	
5. How was this spent?	
6. What analysis do you carry out to help you decide what training and development is needed?	
7. What are your expectations of your managers and departmental employees?	
8. How do you communicate these expectations to the people concerned?	
9. How do you monitor to see if people achieve your expectations?	
10. What happens when people do achieve your expectations?	

99

Reproduced from *Training Needs Analysis Toolkit,* Sharon Bartram and
Brenda Gibson, Gower, Aldershot, 1995

? *Exercise 10.2 (concluded)*

QUESTIONS	KEY POINTS
11. What happens when people do not achieve your expectations?	
12. What will your department look like in five years' time?	
13. What knowledge and skill will be needed: • at your level • at other levels?	
14. Which of these do you already possess: • at your level • at other levels?	
15. Which of these will need to be developed: • at your level • at other levels?	
16. How do you identify potential?	
17. How do you prepare people for change?	
18. What types of learning opportunities do you offer: • external courses • in-house courses • projects • on-the-job coaching?	
19. What are the priorities in training and development for the next twelve months?	
20. Why?	

Reproduced from *Training Needs Analysis Toolkit,* Sharon Bartram and
Brenda Gibson, Gower, Aldershot, 1995

Exercise 10.3: Managers Managing Supervisors (or Equivalent)

QUESTIONS	KEY POINTS
1. What link do you see between your departmental objectives and training and development?	
2. Is training and development viewed as an investment or a cost?	
3. How much authority do you have in recommending spending on training and development?	
4. What type of training and development have you arranged in the past twelve months: • for yourself • for your employees?	
5. What indicators do you use to check the results of this training and development?	
6. What analysis do you carry out to help you decide what training and development is needed?	
7. What are your expectations of your employees?	
8. How do you communicate these expectations to the people concerned?	
9. How do you monitor to see if people achieve your expectations?	
10. What happens when people do achieve your expectations?	

101

Reproduced from *Training Needs Analysis Toolkit,* Sharon Bartram and Brenda Gibson, Gower, Aldershot, 1995

? *Exercise 10.3 (concluded)*

QUESTIONS	KEY POINTS
11. What happens when people do not achieve your expectations?	
12. What will your department look like in five years' time?	
13. What knowledge and skill will be needed: • at your level • at other levels?	
14. Which of these do you already possess: • at your level • at other levels?	
15. Which of these will need to be developed: • at your level • at other levels?	
16. How do you identify potential?	
17. How do you prepare people for change?	
18. What types of learning opportunities do you offer: • external courses • in-house courses • projects • on-the-job coaching?	
19. What are the priorities in training and development for the next twelve months?	
20. Why?	

102

Reproduced from *Training Needs Analysis Toolkit,* Sharon Bartram and
Brenda Gibson, Gower, Aldershot, 1995

Exercise 10.4:   First-Line Managers/Supervisors (or Equivalent)

QUESTIONS	KEY POINTS
1. What link do you see between your objectives and training and development?	
2. Is training and development viewed as an investment or a cost?	
3. How much authority do you have in recommending spending on training and development?	
4. What training and development have you arranged in the past twelve months?	
5. What indicators do you use to check the results of this training and development?	
6. What analysis do you carry out to help you decide what training and development is needed?	
7. What are your expectations of your employees?	
8. How do you communicate these expectations to the people concerned?	
9. How do you monitor to see if people achieve your expectations?	
10. What happens when people do achieve your expectations?	

Reproduced from *Training Needs Analysis Toolkit,* Sharon Bartram and
Brenda Gibson, Gower, Aldershot, 1995

? *Exercise 10.4 (concluded)*

QUESTIONS	KEY POINTS
11. What happens when people do not achieve your expectations?	
12. What will your department look like in five years' time?	
13. What knowledge and skill will be needed: • at your level • at other levels?	
14. Which of these do you already possess: • at your level • at other levels?	
15. Which of these will need to be developed: • at your level • at other levels?	
16. What is your role in identifying potential?	
17. How do you prepare people for change?	
18. How much of your time is spent coaching people in their workplace?	
19. What are your priorities in training and development for the next twelve months?	
20. Why?	

104

Reproduced from *Training Needs Analysis Toolkit,* Sharon Bartram and Brenda Gibson, Gower, Aldershot, 1995

Exercise 10.5: Other Employee Grades

QUESTIONS	KEY POINTS
1. What training and development have you had in the last twelve months?	
2. Who carried out this training?	
3. What follow-up has there been?	
4. Is training and development viewed as an investment or a cost?	
5. What involvement do you have in deciding what training and development is made available to you?	
6. Are all your skills being used in your current job?	
7. What skills do you have that could be utilized more effectively?	
8. How do you know what is expected of you in your job?	
9. What happens if you achieve these expectations?	
10. What happens if you do not achieve these expectations?	

105

? *Exercise 10.5 (concluded)*

QUESTIONS	KEY POINTS
11. What will your department/ section look like in five years' time?	
12. What knowledge and skill will you need to do your job then?	
13. Which of these do you already have?	
14. Which of these will you need to develop?	
15. What changes have happened in the recent past?	
16. How did you find out about these changes?	
17. In what ways did the organization prepare you for these changes?	
18. How much of your time is spent training other people?	
19. What are your priorities in training and development for the next twelve months?	
20. Why?	

Reproduced from *Training Needs Analysis Toolkit,* Sharon Bartram and Brenda Gibson, Gower, Aldershot, 1995

C

Managing Resources

This section shows you how to match the current performance of people to the recommended best practice. It is likely that standards are known, so gaps in performance are easily quantifiable. There are seven activities in this section:

11. Personal Assessment
12. Management Match
13. Managing Time
14. Managing People
15. Managing Expenditure
16. How Others See Me
17. How Do I See My Managers?

The target group is anyone who is responsible for managing this range of resources, and one of the most important resources in any organization is its people.

"Personal Assessment" helps people find out how much of their time is devoted to the key elements of managing others.

"Management Match" helps people to discover their own strengths and areas for development in managing themselves and others, as well as checking on what they see as the priorities for the organization.

"Managing Time" highlights the problems people have in this area and helps them to achieve more effective use of their time.

"Managing People" requires the respondents to describe their personal style and approach when managing others. This can then be compared with a benchmark response to identify strengths and areas for development.

"Managing Expenditure" checks current performance against a given set of best practice criteria.

"How Others See Me" uses the powerful process of structured feedback from those who are managed and compares it with how the managers see themselves.

"How Do I See My Managers?" shows senior managers how to assess the competence of managers that report to them. Development needs are ascertained by matching certain characteristics of managing others against actual performance.

107

Managing resources may not be a part of the role of every trainer, so first ask yourself: "Is this my job?" If your answer is *No*, move on to the next section. If your answer is *Yes*, check that you have made the preparations that are necessary to the success of this aspect of training needs analysis. Use the following checklist as your guide.

Preparation	Y	N	*Action*
Have you			
1. Identified and won the support of the appropriate sponsor?			
2. Clarified your objectives — do you know what you want to achieve from using the activity?			
3. Assessed the potential problems of using the activities in this target group and made contingencies for them?			
4. Considered the expectations that taking part will raise and discussed them with your sponsor and other managers?			
5. Practiced your coaching skills as required by a number of the activities? They are: • listening • questioning • seeking contributions • building on proposals			
6. Checked your understanding of what would be the best responses to the activities?			
7. Selected the best method of collecting the information from the options given in the activity?			
8. Prepared your presentation for the target group?			

11

Personal Assessment

Objective

- To find out how much time is spent carrying out key management activities and to assess performance in achieving the desired results. Analyzing this information will indicate where training is necessary to attain organizational, departmental, and personal objectives.

Description

This activity uses an activity log together with an analysis sheet to collect information.

Materials

Sufficient copies of Exercises 11.1 and 11.2.

Collecting Information

Methods	Benefits	Potential problems
Activity log completed individually followed by interview to complete the analysis.	• Easy to administer. • Creates ownership in the user. • Minimal intrusion into user's routine.	Analysis could be time-consuming.
Activity log and analysis completed individually followed by interview to discuss the findings.	• Easy to administer. • Gives the user total control. • Developmental activity in itself.	Level of commitment required by the user.

Methods

A. Activity log completed individually followed by interview to complete the analysis.

1. Explain the purpose of the activity to the target group.
2. Give each person sufficient copies of the activity log (Exercise 11.1) to generate a useful amount of information and agree to a time limit for completion.
3. Arrange and carry out interviews with each person using Exercise 11.2 as the basis for the discussion. At the end of the interview you should have completed Exercise 11.2, which summarizes the person's training needs. Allow at least one and a half hours per interview.

B. Activity log and analysis completed individually followed by interview to discuss the findings.

1. Explain the purpose of the activity to the target group.
2. Give each person sufficient copies of the activity log (Exercise 11.1) to generate a useful amount of information, and a copy of document 11.2 to analyze the findings. Agree to a time limit for completion.
3. Arrange and carry out interviews with each person using Exercise 11.2 as the basis for the discussion. At the end of the interview you should have found out enough information from the person to confirm their training needs. Allow at least one hour per interview.

Whichever option you choose, use the analysis document to determine which activities are performed most often by an individual but that are perceived by them as needing development. These are likely to be priority training needs. The next level of priority will be those activities that the person occasionally carries out and again where they rate their performance as needing development. Look at the activities the person carries out only occasionally or never but that are an important part of managing effectively, then draw up a personal development plan for future action.

Exercise 11.1: Activity Log

Use this sheet to log the activities you do during your working day. To find out how much time you are spending on these activities, write a checkmark (✓) to represent each fifteen minutes spent on the activity that best describes what you are doing. At the end of each day, total up the number of checkmarks against each activity and convert this into real time.

Activity	Day one	Day two	Day three	Day four	Day five
Maintaining and improving the quality of what we do					
Implementing change to the way things are done					
Controlling resources other than people					
Recruiting and selecting staff					
Developing people, including self					
Allocating tasks and monitoring results					
Developing effective working relationships					
Dealing with information					
Solving problems and making decisions					
Other (please specify)					
Total					

111

Reproduced from *Training Needs Analysis Toolkit,* Sharon Bartram and Brenda Gibson, Gower, Aldershot, 1995

Exercise 11.2: Analyzing the Activity Log

Use the information from your log to indicate how often you do each of the activities and to rate your performance. Select *Often*, *Occasionally*, or *Never* to indicate frequency. Select a performance rating of X for excellent, C for competent, or D for needs developing. You should have two checkmarks (✓) for each activity.

Activity	Often	Occasionally	Never	X	C	D
Maintaining and improving the quality of what we do						
Implementing change to the way things are done						
Controlling resources other than people						
Recruiting and selecting staff						
Developing people, including self						
Allocating tasks and monitoring results						
Developing effective working relationships						
Dealing with information						
Solving problems and making decisions						
Other (please specify)						

113

Reproduced from *Training Needs Analysis Toolkit,* Sharon Bartram and Brenda Gibson, Gower, Aldershot, 1995

12

Management Match

Objectives

- To discover strengths and areas for improvement in ten managerial and supervisory activities.
- To compare the needs of the organization with the skills of its managers and supervisors.
- To develop training plans for individuals and groups.

Description

This activity uses a card sort approach to extract information.

Materials

1. Sufficient supply of Exercise 12.1 cut and pasted onto cards and organized into packs. (You may also paste the sheet on cardboard and cut.)
2. Sufficient copies of Exercise 12.2.
3. Exercise 12.3.
4. A meeting room.

Collecting Information

Methods	Benefits	Potential problems
Group activity with a mix of seniority levels.	• Clearer picture of entire organizational training needs. • Sharing of perceptions about what is important to the organization.	• Difficult to arrange. • Fear of disclosure.
Group activity on a departmental basis.	Clearer picture of departmental training needs.	• Fear of disclosure. • Disruption to working routines.

Methods	Benefits	Potential problems
Group activity with similar levels of seniority across all areas.	Able to target training more accurately.	• Fear of disclosure. • Availability of individuals.
Individually structured interviews.	• Identifies specific training needs and individuals with potential. • Non-threatening. • Limits disruption to work.	Time-consuming.
Separately structured interviews with individuals and their managers followed by joint discussion.	• Opportunity to give and receive feedback on performance. Wins the commitment of the manager to the training plan. • Identifies specific training needs and individuals with potential.	• Time-consuming. • Overlap with an appraisal procedure that might be in use.

Methods

A. Group activity (first three methods).

1. Explain the purpose of the activity to the target group.
2. Hold a meeting with the group, allowing at least two hours.
3. Give each person a pack of cards cut up from Exercise 12.1 and a copy of Exercise 12.2, their personal assessment sheet. Allow sufficient time for each person to sort the cards and record their responses.
4. Leave one pack of cards with the group and collect the rest.
5. Ask the group to agree on the top ten priorities for the organization and to record their selections onto their own personal assessment sheet (Exercise 12.2).
6. Allow sufficient time for each person to reflect on their personal strengths and areas for improvement, matching these with the priorities for the organization, and to write their comments about how best to utilize and enhance their capabilities onto Exercise 12.2.
7. Take a copy of each completed Exercise 12.2 and explain that they will be used to compile an overall findings sheet in order to discover the priority training needs of the group and to form the basis of the feedback they will receive.

B. Individual structured interviews.

1. Explain the purpose of the activity to the target group.
2. Arrange separate interviews with each person, allowing approximately one hour per interview.
3. Give each person a pack of cards cut up from Exercise 12.1 and ask them to arrange them into three piles: their top ten strengths in priority order; their top ten areas for improvement in priority order; and a pile to be discarded.
4. Record their choices onto a personal assessment sheet (Exercise 12.2).
5. Reshuffle the pack of cards and ask the person to arrange two piles: the top ten areas of most importance to the organization, in priority order; and a pile to be discarded.
6. Record their choices onto Exercise 12.2 and discuss them. Ask them to comment on how their capabilities can be utilized and enhanced. Record their comments onto Exercise 12.2.
7. Give a copy of the completed Exercise 12.2 to the person and explain that the overall findings will form the basis of feedback to them about training plans.

C. Separate structured interviews with individuals and their managers followed by joint discussion.

Follow steps 1 to 6 as described for the individually structured interviews.

7. Repeat these steps with the individual's manager, asking the manager to prioritize the strengths and areas for improvement as he or she sees them in their staff member.
8. Arrange a meeting between the individual, their manager, and yourself to discuss their findings and agree on the training needs to be addressed.

Trainer's Notes: Management Actions — Card Reference

Motivation
1. Encouraging my team to take a real interest in their jobs.
2. Encouraging good work habits and discouraging those that are not productive.
3. Dealing with the individual who has the ability but does not do a good job.
4. Persuading my team to use their initiative, seeing what has to be done and doing it without being told.

Delegation
5. Knowing what to do myself and knowing what to delegate to others.
6. Dealing with individuals who are anxious to take on more responsibility which I know they can't handle.
7. Dealing with individuals who could take on more responsibility but don't want it.
8. Allowing my team sufficient latitude to decide what to do and how to do it.

Dealing with problems
9. Choosing the best of several alternative ways of doing a job.
10. Identifying the real problem in a difficult situation.
11. Organizing a complicated problem into manageable tasks.
12. Making decisions when necessary to do so.

Training
13. Assessing whether my team members know how to do their jobs.
14. Measuring the effects of the training my team receives to ensure it is working.
15. Training my team using a logical step-by-step approach.
16. Identifying training needs among my team.

Performance
17. Setting achievable standards for myself and others.
18. Evaluating my own and others' performance fairly.
19. Correcting poor performance promptly and effectively.
20. Helping others with personal problems that affect their job performance.

119

Reproduced from *Training Needs Analysis Toolkit,* Sharon Bartram and
Brenda Gibson, Gower, Aldershot, 1995

Trainer's Notes (concluded)

Planning

21. Planning the work of my team.
22. Monitoring work progress against the plan.
23. Anticipating problems that might block the work's progress.
24. Using the resources of my team effectively by assigning work appropriately to individuals.

Time

25. Coaching my team to help them make better use of their time.
26. Dealing with the excessive demands placed upon my time by other people.
27. Using my time effectively each day.
28. Keeping my demands on other people's time to a level appropriate for the job.

Ideas

29. Generating suggestions from my team.
30. Handling poor or bad suggestions from others in a way that does not discourage them.
31. Encouraging my team's commitment and cooperation to new ways of working.
32. Selling new ideas to my manager.

Teamwork

33. Helping the individuals in my area to work effectively as a team.
34. Dealing with conflict between individuals whose personalities clash.
35. Dealing with individuals who don't carry their share of the load.
36. Ensuring effective relations between my team and others so that we work smoothly together.

Communication

37. Communicating clearly what I expect from my team.
38. Giving instructions to others to achieve the results I want.
39. Creating effective communications with my manager.
40. Conducting effective meetings with others.

Reproduced from *Training Needs Analysis Toolkit*, Sharon Bartram and Brenda Gibson, Gower, Aldershot, 1995

Exercise 12.1: Management Action Cards

1. Encouraging my team to take a real interest in their jobs.	2. Encouraging good work habits and discouraging those that are not productive.
3. Dealing with the individual who has the ability but does not do a good job.	4. Persuading my team to use their initiative — seeing what has to be done and doing it without being told.
5. Knowing what to do myself and knowing what to delegate to others.	6. Dealing with individuals who are anxious to take on more responsibility which I know they can't handle.
7. Dealing with individuals who could take more responsibility but don't want it.	8. Allowing my team sufficient latitude to decide what to do and how to do it.
9. Choosing the best of several alternative ways of doing a job.	10. Identifying the real problem in a difficult situation.

Reproduced from *Training Needs Analysis Toolkit,* Sharon Bartram and
Brenda Gibson, Gower, Aldershot, 1995

11. Organizing a complicated problem into manageable tasks.	12. Making decisions when necessary to do so.
13. Assessing whether my team members know how to do their jobs.	14. Measuring the effects of the training my team receives to ensure it is working.
15. Training my team using a logical step-by-step approach.	16. Identifying training needs among my team.
17. Setting achievable standards for myself and others.	18. Evaluating my own and others' performance fairly.
19. Correcting poor performance promptly and effectively.	20. Helping others with personal problems that affect their job performance.

21. Planning the work of my team.	22. Monitoring work progress against the plan.
23. Anticipating problems that might block the work's progress.	24. Using the resources of my team effectively by assigning work appropriately to individuals.
25. Coaching my team to help them make better use of their time.	26. Dealing with the excessive demands placed upon my time by other people.
27. Using my time effectively each day.	28. Keeping my demands on other people's time to a level appropriate for the job.
29. Generating suggestions from my team.	30. Handling poor or bad suggestions from others in a way that does not discourage them.

Reproduced from *Training Needs Analysis Toolkit,* Sharon Bartram and
Brenda Gibson, Gower, Aldershot, 1995

31. Encouraging my team's commitment and cooperation to new ways of working.	32. Selling new ideas to my manager.
33. Helping the individuals in my area to work effectively as a team.	34. Dealing with conflict between individuals whose personalities clash.
35. Dealing with individuals who don't carry their share of the load.	36. Ensuring effective relations between my team and others so that we work smoothly together.
37. Communicating clearly what I expect from my team.	38. Giving instructions to others to achieve the results I want.
39. Creating effective communications with my manager.	40. Conducting effective meetings with others.

Exercise 12.2: Personal Assessment Sheet

My top ten strengths:	My top ten areas for improvement:	The top ten priorities for the organization:
1.	1.	1.
2.	2.	2.
3.	3.	3.
4.	4.	4.
5.	5.	5.
6.	6.	6.
7.	7.	7.
8.	8.	8.
9.	9.	9.
10.	10.	10.

Action:

Exercise 12.3: Summary of Findings

Card number	Times selected as top ten priority for organization	Times selected as top ten strength	Times selected as top ten improvement need	Training need (yes/no)	Training options
1 Motivation					
2					
3					
4					
5 Delegation					
6					
7					
8					
9 Problems					
10					
11					
12					
13 Training					
14					
15					
16					
17 Performance					
18					
19					
20					

127

Reproduced from *Training Needs Analysis Toolkit,* Sharon Bartram and
Brenda Gibson, Gower, Aldershot, 1995

Card number	Times selected as top ten priority for organization	Times selected as top ten strength	Times selected as top ten improvement need	Training need (yes/no)	Training options
Planning 21					
22					
23					
24					
Time 25					
26					
27					
28					
Ideas 29					
30					
31					
32					
Teamwork 33					
34					
35					
36					
Communication37					
38					
39					
40					

Reproduced from *Training Needs Analysis Toolkit,* Sharon Bartram and Brenda Gibson, Gower, Aldershot, 1995

13

Managing Time

Objectives

- To identify aspects of self-organization requiring improvement in order to increase the effectiveness of the individual's job performance.
- To discover any underlying organizational issues that may be manifesting themselves as symptoms of poor time management.

Description

This activity is a survey for individuals to complete. It can be adapted into a card sort as an alternative method of gathering information.

Materials

1. Sufficient copies of Exercise 13.1.
2. A meeting room.
3. Flipchart paper and pens.

Collecting Information

Methods	Benefits	Potential problems
Survey completed individually followed by individual interviews.	• Easy to administer. • Everyone will have their own development plan.	• Misses the opportunity to identify trends. • Time consuming to analyze.
Survey completed individually followed by group discussions, either on a departmental basis or across departments.	• Easy to administer. • Trends will be identified.	• Some individuals' training needs may be missed. • Difficulty in bringing groups together.

Methods

A. Survey completed individually followed by individual interviews.
1. Explain the purpose of the activity to the target group.
2. Give each person a copy of Exercise 13.1 and agree to a time limit for completion.
3. Arrange an interview with each person, allowing up to one hour per interview.
4. Discuss the results of the survey and write down the top five priorities.
5. Coach the individual to find ways of overcoming the problems.
6. Explain that their information will be the basis for an action plan in the form of a matrix showing trends and development needs.

B. Survey completed individually followed by group discussions, either on a departmental basis or across departments.
Follow steps 1 and 2 above.

3. Arrange group discussions, allowing one and a half hours for each group.
4. Using a prepared flipchart displaying the 20 statements from Exercise 13.1, ask each person to place a red checkmark (✓) against their most important statement and a black checkmark against their other four choices.
5. Encourage the group to analyze the findings, concentrating on how their jobs are affected and how the organization is affected.
6. Explain that their information will be the basis for an action plan in the form of a matrix to show trends and development needs.

For whichever method is chosen, it will be helpful to explain that the statements on the survey fall into the following categories:

Category	Statement(s)
Personal disorganization	1, 2
Lack of discipline	3, 4, 5, 6
Lack of priorities	7, 8
Reading	9
Interruptions — telephone	10, 11
Interruptions — unexpected visitors	12, 13
Inability to say *no*	14, 15
Inability to finish work	16, 17
Indecision and delay	18, 19, 20

Exercise 13.1: Managing Time

Please read each of the 20 statements and place a checkmark (✓) in either the *Yes* or *No* column if the statement describes you in your workplace.

		YES	NO
1.	I don't have a routine or system for organizing my time.		
2.	I have a fear of forgetting things.		
3.	I don't set performance standards.		
4.	I lack direction in my work.		
5.	I don't always follow up on work.		
6.	I tend to respond to urgent matters, postponing what is important.		
7.	I don't have time to plan.		
8.	I would rather be doing than thinking.		
9.	I have no priorities for what to read and how thoroughly.		
10.	I tend to make unstructured telephone calls.		
11.	I don't prioritize, so all telephone calls are put through to me.		
12.	I don't avoid having drop-in visitors.		
13.	I find it difficult to bring visits to a close.		
14.	I like to feel important and involved in everything.		
15.	I don't know how to say *No* and fear offending someone.		
16.	I lack an overview and perspective to my work.		
17.	I suffer from setting unrealistic time estimates and lack of deadlines.		
18.	I don't like making decisions for fear of what might happen if mistakes are made.		
19.	I don't always anticipate the effects of my decisions.		
20.	I suffer from an ineffective approach to making decisions.		

From the statements checkmarked *Yes*, select the top five that have the biggest impact on how effective you are in your job. Try to rank the five in order of importance:

Biggest impact.   1.
                  2.
                  3.
                  4.
                  5.

14

Managing People

Objectives

- To help newly appointed managers to develop management of their teams.
- To highlight the training needs of individuals in managing others prior to appointment as first-line managers.
- To assess the competence of individuals in managing others when they have received no previous formal training.

Description

This activity consists of a series of open-ended statements that allow individuals to describe their methods of working when managing people. Their replies are matched to a suggested checklist of benchmark responses. This benchmark can be adapted to suit the organization.

Materials

1. Sufficient copies of Exercise 14.1.
2. Exercise 14.2.

Collecting Information

Methods	Benefits	Potential problems
Completed individually followed by individual interviews.	• Each person will have a specific development plan. • Trends can be incorporated into training courses for groups of people. • Answers can be clarified.	Time-consuming in analysis.

Methods	Benefits	Potential problems
Mail survey.	• Easy to administer. • Speeds up analysis.	• Percentage of surveys not returned. • Ambiguous answers not clarified.

Methods

A. Completed individually followed by individual interviews.
1. Explain the purpose of the activity to the target group.
2. Give each person a copy of Exercise 14.1 and agree to a time limit for completion.
3. Arrange an interview with each person, allowing at least one hour per interview.
4. Discuss their responses, checking how closely they match the benchmark checklist (Exercise 14.2). Write down gaps in knowledge as potential training needs.
5. Explain that the information in their responses will form the basis for an action plan. Take a copy of the completed document for further analysis.
6. Develop a matrix to show how each individual matches the benchmark checklist (Exercise 14.2).

B. Mail survey.
Follow steps 1, 2, 5, and 6 as above.

Exercise 14.1: Managing People

Please complete the following sentences as fully as possible:

1. When deciding my future personnel requirements, the considerations I take into account are:

2. When selecting a new person as a member of my team, the factors I take into account are:

3. The ways in which I develop and improve the performance of my team are:

4. The steps I take to discover appropriate activities to develop the individuals in my team are:

5. The ways in which I improve my own job performance are:

Reproduced from *Training Needs Analysis Toolkit,* Sharon Bartram and Brenda Gibson, Gower, Aldershot, 1995

? *Exercise 14.1 (continued)*

6. When setting work objectives, the factors I take into account are:

7. In order to achieve these objectives, I plan activities and determine work methods in the following way:

8. The steps I take when allocating work are:

9. The methods I use to measure the results achieved by my team, the individuals in the team, and me are:

10. To ensure that my feedback to people concerning their performance is effective, the steps I take are:

11. To win and keep the trust and support of my staff, the steps I take are:

136

Reproduced from *Training Needs Analysis Toolkit,* Sharon Bartram and
Brenda Gibson, Gower, Aldershot, 1995

12. To win and keep the trust and support of my manager, the steps I take are:

13. To build relationships with work colleagues, the steps I take are:

14. To deal with interpersonal conflict, the methods I use are:

15. When using the discipline or grievance procedure, the factors I take into account are:

16. When a member of my team has a personal problem that is affecting their work, the steps I take are:

137

Reproduced from *Training Needs Analysis Toolkit,* Sharon Bartram and Brenda Gibson, Gower, Aldershot, 1995

Exercise 14.2: Benchmark Checklist

Sentence	Benchmark response
1.	Strengths and weaknesses of current team Needs of the department and organization Quantifiable information on current team, for example: age range, task coverage, succession plans Legislation on equal opportunity policies Financial constraints.
2.	Evidence from the prospective employee of skills appropriate to the requirements of the job The organization's selection criteria Legislation on sex discrimination and race relations The balance of skills and qualities the prospective employee will bring to the existing team.
3.	Maintain up-to-date information on strengths and weaknesses of team members Encourage individuals to set realistic objectives for themselves Match individual's talents to assignments Provide opportunities for formal training Use coaching as a way of developing people on a daily basis Give regular constructive feedback on results achieved.
4.	Match individual's talents to assignments Encourage individuals to evaluate their own learning and developmental needs Analyze activities to clarify the opportunities they present.
5.	Set for myself achievable, realistic, and challenging objectives Review my performance regularly with my manager Review my performance regularly with my team.
6.	The objectives can be achieved The objectives do not conflict with other commitments Communicate clearly the objectives to those concerned and to verify understanding of what is expected The methods to use to monitor progress Defining a mixture of short-, medium-, and long-term objectives.
7.	Assess the amount of supervision each individual will require Seek contributions from individuals on how the objectives can be achieved Ensure the activities and work methods will provide developmental opportunities Ensure the activities and work methods are in line with the organization's way of working Make the best use of resources available.
8.	Use the strengths of the team most effectively Clearly define responsibilities and limits of authority Provide individuals with learning opportunities Clearly communicate expectations and verify understanding Be available for ongoing guidance as requested by the team and individuals.
9.	Monitor progress and take appropriate actions, for example: praise good performance; and give constructive feedback to improve performance Define quantifiable measures, for example: quality, quantity, time frames, as part of objectives and note performance against these.
10.	Give feedback in sufficient detail that it can be acted upon Use observed examples, not opinions Praise good performance as well as highlighting areas for improvement Give feedback at the appropriate time and place.

Reproduced from *Training Needs Analysis Toolkit,* Sharon Bartram and Brenda Gibson, Gower, Aldershot, 1995

? *Exercise 14.2 (concluded)*

Sentence	Benchmark response
11.	Listen to the views of the team and individuals Encourage contributions from the team and individuals Keep the team and individuals regularly informed Be consistent in praising good performance and highlighting areas for improvement Carry out undertakings given to team and individuals Give reasons if ideas and suggestions are not implemented.
12.	Keep my manager regularly informed Meet the standards expected of me Seek information from my manager as appropriate Do not allow disagreements to spoil the relationship Present proposals for action supported by quantifiable justifications Accept refusal of proposals by asking for reasons and amending proposals appropriately.
13.	Carry out promises and undertakings Deal with differences of opinion in a way that maintains respect Freely exchange opinions and information Encourage open and honest behavior by setting a good example Listen to colleagues.
14.	Clearly communicate the standards of work and behavior expected Provide regular opportunities for people to discuss problems Take prompt action to deal with potential and actual conflict.
15.	Ensure that my team members are kept informed of the procedures Use the procedures at the appropriate times Be impartial in applying the procedures Take notes and record details when using the procedures.
16.	Find a private place to discuss the situation with the person Listen and provide feedback so that he/she takes responsibility for finding solutions Monitor the situation to ensure a positive outcome.

140

Reproduced from *Training Needs Analysis Toolkit,* Sharon Bartram and
Brenda Gibson, Gower, Aldershot, 1995

15

Managing Expenditure

Objectives

- To identify ways of improving the processes and techniques used in managing expenditure.
- To discover the degree to which best practice is currently followed when managing expenditure.
- To determine specific expenditure techniques required by managers.

Description

This activity is a survey that combines a series of statements describing best practice with a list of techniques useful in managing expenditure.

Materials

1. Sufficient copies of Exercise 15.1.
2. One copy of Exercise 15.2.
3. Meeting room.

Collecting Information

Methods	Benefits	Potential problems
Mailed survey.	• Easy to administer. • Information generated quickly.	• Percentage of surveys not returned. • Unable to verify understanding of respondents.
Individually completed followed by individual interviews.	• Able to verify understanding of participants.	Time-consuming.

Methods

A. Mailed survey.
 1. Explain the purpose of the activity to the target group.
 2. Distribute one copy of the survey (Exercise 15.1) to each person asking them to make a copy of their responses before returning the completed survey.
 3. Agree to a time limit for completion.
 4. Analyze the completed surveys using Exercise 15.2 and report the findings back to the target group.

B. Individual interviews.
 1. Explain the purpose of the activity to the target group.
 2. Distribute one copy of the survey (Exercise 15.1) to each person and agree to a time and date for the interview.
 3. Allow at least 30 minutes per interview.
 4. Take a copy of each completed survey and analyze them using Exercise 15.2.
 5. Report the findings to the target group.

Exercise 15.1: Managing Expenditure

Please read the following statements carefully and then place a checkmark (✓) to indicate whether you do this always, frequently, sometimes, or never.

Statements	Always	Frequently	Sometimes	Never
Budgeting expenditure				
I gather information from internal and external sources to develop recommendations for expenditure.				
I seek input from the appropriate people to develop my recommendations.				
The benefits to be derived from the expenditure are clearly stated in my recommendations.				
I present my recommendations in a clear and concise way.				
I compare the actual expenditure with the recommendations to make improvements in the future.				
Controlling expenditure				
I ensure that everyone in my team knows how they can contribute to controlling resources.				
I keep expenditure within established budgets.				
I acknowledge when I have to refer requests for expenditure to other people and act promptly.				
I keep accurate, legible, and complete records.				
When I see ways of increasing efficiency, I quickly pass on my recommendations to the appropriate people.				
I correctly interpret information about costs and the utilization of resources.				
I take corrective action promptly to minimize the effect of any deviations from expenditure plans.				

To assist me in managing expenditure I would like to know more about the following techniques. (Place a checkmark ✓ in the boxes provided to indicate your choices. Spaces have been left for you to add any techniques not mentioned in these lists.)

Trend analysis		Balance sheets		
Zero-based budgeting		Profit and loss		
Life-cycle budgeting		Value analysis		
Depreciation		Break-even analysis		
Cash flow		Cost-benefit analysis		

143

Exercise 15.2: Managing Expenditure — Analysis

Statements	No. of times always selected	No. of times frequently selected	No. of times sometimes selected	No. of times never selected	Consequences
Budgeting expenditure I gather information from internal and external sources to develop recommendations for expenditure.					
I seek input from the appropriate people to develop my recommendations.					
The benefits to be derived from the expenditure are clearly stated in my recommendations.					
I present my recommendations in a clear and concise way.					
I compare the actual expenditure with the recommendations to make improvements in the future.					
Controlling expenditure I ensure that everyone in my team knows how they can contribute to controlling resources.					
I keep expenditure within established budgets.					
I acknowledge when I have to refer requests for expenditure to other people and act promptly.					
I keep accurate, legible, and complete records.					
When I see ways of increasing efficiency, I quickly pass on my recommendations to the appropriate people.					
I correctly interpret information about costs and the utilization of resources.					
I take corrective action promptly to minimize the effect of any deviations from expenditure plans.					

Technique	No. of times selected	Technique	No. of times selected	Technique	No. of times selected
Trend analysis		Balance sheets			
Zero-based budgeting		Profit and loss			
Life-cycle budgeting		Value analysis			
Depreciation		Break-even analysis			
Cash flow		Cost-benefit analysis			

145

Reproduced from *Training Needs Analysis Toolkit*, Sharon Bartram and Brenda Gibson, Gower, Aldershot, 1995

16

How Others See Me

Objectives

- To compare the perceptions managers have of themselves of how they are working with their teams to the perceptions of their team members.
- To pinpoint areas of leadership and teamworking to develop in light of this comparison.

Description

This activity is a survey that uses a rating scale to measure perceptions of management performance.

Materials

1. Sufficient copies of Exercises 16.1 — 16.3.
2. A meeting room.

Collecting Information

Methods	Benefits	Potential problems
Manager and all team members complete survey with follow-up interviews.	All views of team members will be taken into account.	• Readiness of managers to accept feedback. • Readiness of team members to give feedback.
Managers and representative team members complete survey with follow-up interviews.	Less time needed for analysis of information	• Views of sample could be unrepresentative. • Readiness of manager to accept feedback.

Methods

A. Manager and all team members complete survey with follow-up interviews.

1. Explain to the managers and their team members the purpose and method of the activity and gain commitment to the approach.
2. Explain to the target group of managers the process of accepting feedback, stressing the important steps: be prepared to listen; be prepared to evaluate, not judge the feedback; be prepared to look for the positive and not recrimination.
3. Distribute a copy of Exercise 16.1 to each manager. Check for understanding and agree to a time limit for completion.
4. Tell the team members to respond as honestly as they can, stressing that confidentiality will be maintained.
5. Distribute a copy of Exercise 16.2 to each person and agree to a time limit for completion.
6. Collect the surveys from the team members and work out an average rating against each statement from their total responses.
7. Arrange a meeting with each manager, allowing at least one hour per meeting.
8. Ask the manager to write down in Column B of their survey the average rating for each statement as generated by their team members.
9. Use Exercise 16.3 to explain the areas of teamwork and leadership referred to in the survey and give the exercise to the manager for future reference. Compare the manager's view of him/herself with the perceptions of their team members, paying particular attention to: areas of agreement where all involved feel that improvement is required and areas where there are differences of opinion and why this might be. Encourage the manager to identify actions that would positively influence the situation. Notes can be made in Column C of Exercise 16.1.
10. Take a copy of the completed Exercise 16.1 to analyze trends and develop a consolidated action plan. Report back to the target group of managers and their team members.

B. Manager and sample of team members complete survey with follow-up interviews.

Follow all the steps above, substituting a sample of team members for the whole team. Select the sample according to the size of the team, the levels of authority, and responsibilities represented in the roles within the team.

Exercise 16.1: Manager's Copy

Consider the way you work with your team by reading the statements and rating how you match them. Using a scale of 0–5 with 5 as the highest, enter your rating in Column A. You will be able to complete Columns B and C at a summary meeting.

Statements	A How I see myself	B How my team sees me	C Actions
1. I go out of my way to encourage people in the group.			
2. I become impatient with people who "beat about the bush."			
3. I urge the group to stick to plans and meet deadlines.			
4. When there are different opinions within the group, I encourage people to talk their differences through to an acceptable agreement.			
5. I can be counted on to suggest original ideas.			
6. I use humor to ease tensions and maintain good relationships.			
7. I look for common understanding before making decisions.			
8. I listen carefully to what others have to say.			
9. I avoid becoming involved in conflicts.			
10. I can quickly see what is wrong with unsound ideas presented by others.			
11. I keep everyone informed about the whys and wherefores of a situation.			
12. I am always ready to back a suggestion for the common good.			
13. I tend to present plenty of ideas.			
14. I draw people out if I sense they have something to contribute.			
15. When there are problems I push ahead and finish the job.			
16. I develop other people's ideas and improve them.			
17. I change my mind after listening to other people's points of view.			
18. I tend to seek approval and support from others.			
19. I don't mind being unpopular if it gets the job done.			
20. I go out of my way to seek ideas and opinions from other people.			
21. I am a friendly person and mix well with others.			
22. I am careful not to jump to conclusions.			

149

Reproduced from *Training Needs Analysis Toolkit,* Sharon Bartram and Brenda Gibson, Gower, Aldershot, 1995

? *Exercise 16.1 (concluded)*

	Statements	A How I see myself	B How my team sees me	C Actions
23.	I am good at noticing when someone in the group is feeling resentful.			
24.	I enjoy analyzing situations and weighing alternatives.			
25.	I can work well with a very wide range of people.			
26.	I have a no-nonsense style.			
27.	I like to "oil the wheels" to help people work well.			
28.	I tend to be forceful and energetic.			
29.	I like to see problems coming and prepare for them.			
30.	I press for action to make sure people don't waste time or go around in circles.			
31.	I can usually persuade people to agree on a course of action.			
32.	When people have second thoughts, I urge them to press on with the task at hand.			
33.	I like to ponder alternatives before making up my mind.			
34.	I tend to be open about how I'm feeling.			
35.	People sometimes think I'm being too analytical and cautious.			
36.	In discussions I like to come straight to the point.			
37.	While I'm interested in all views, I don't hesitate to make up my mind when a decision has to be made.			
38.	Flippant people irritate me.			
39.	I am able to influence people without harassing them.			
40.	I like to think through ideas before acting on them.			

150

Reproduced from *Training Needs Analysis Toolkit,* Sharon Bartram and Brenda Gibson, Gower, Aldershot, 1995

Exercise 16.2: Team Member's Copy

Think about how your manager works with you and the rest of the team. Read the statements and enter your rating in the box provided, using a scale of 0–5, with 5 as the highest.

Statements	Rating
1. They go out of their way to encourage people in the group.	
2. They become impatient with people who "'beat about the bush."	
3. They urge the group to stick to plans and meet deadlines.	
4. When there are different opinions within the group, they encourage people to talk their differences through to an acceptable agreement.	
5. They can be counted on to suggest original ideas.	
6. They use humor to ease tensions and maintain good relationships.	
7. They look for common understanding before making decisions.	
8. They listen carefully to what others have to say.	
9. They avoid becoming involved in conflicts.	
10. They can quickly see what is wrong with unsound ideas presented by others.	
11. They keep everyone informed about the whys and wherefores of a situation.	
12. They are always ready to back a suggestion for the common good.	
13. They tend to present plenty of ideas.	
14. They draw people out if they sense they have something to contribute.	
15. When there are problems they push ahead and get the job done.	
16. They develop other people's ideas and improve them.	
17. They change their mind after listening to other people's points of view.	
18. They tend to seek approval and support from others.	
19. They don't mind being unpopular if it gets the job done.	
20. They go out of their way to seek ideas and opinions from other people.	
21. They are friendly and mix well with others.	
22. They are careful not to jump to conclusions.	
23. They are good at noticing when someone in the group is feeling resentful.	

151

Reproduced from *Training Needs Analysis Toolkit,* Sharon Bartram and Brenda Gibson, Gower, Aldershot, 1995

Statements	Rating
24. They enjoy analyzing situations and weighing alternatives.	
25. They can work well with a very wide range of people.	
26. They have a no-nonsense style.	
27. They like to "oil the wheels" to help people work well.	
28. They tend to be forceful and energetic.	
29. They like to see problems coming and prepare for them.	
30. They press for action to make sure people don't waste time or go around in circles.	
31. They can usually persuade people to agree on a course of action.	
32. When people have second thoughts, they urge them to press on with the task at hand.	
33. They like to ponder alternatives before making up their mind.	
34. They tend to be open about how they're feeling.	
35. People sometimes think they're being too analytical and cautious.	
36. In discussions they like to come straight to the point.	
37. While they're interested in all views, they don't hesitate to make up their mind when a decision has to be made.	
38. Flippant people irritate them.	
39. They are able to influence people without harassing them.	
40. They like to think through ideas before acting on them.	

Exercise 16.3: Summary

The statements can be arranged under four headings:

1. How you see yourself as a leader.
2. How you see yourself as someone who finishes the job.
3. How you see yourself as someone who can analyze and generate ideas.
4. How you see yourself as a team builder.

Transfer your ratings onto the key below and add the combined ratings of the members of your team for comparison.

KEY

Item	Me	Team	Item	Me	Team	Item	Me	Team	Item	Me	Team
1			2			5			6		
4			3			10			9		
7			15			13			12		
8			19			16			17		
11			26			22			18		
14			28			24			21		
20			30			29			23		
31			32			33			25		
37			36			35			27		
39			38			40			34		
Total			**Total**			**Total**			**Total**		
LEADER			DOER			IDEAS			BUILDER		

Actions I will take as a result of this analysis:

153

Reproduced from *Training Needs Analysis Toolkit,* Sharon Bartram and Brenda Gibson, Gower, Aldershot, 1995

17

How Do I See My Managers?

Objective

- To develop departmental management development plans.

Description

By working through a series of statements, this activity helps senior managers to identify the characteristics collectively displayed by their own managers. The process highlights both team and individual development needs.

Materials

1. Sufficient copies of Exercises 17.1 and 17.2.
2. A meeting room.

Collecting Information

Methods	Benefits	Potential problems
Senior manager completes the survey individually followed by individual meeting.	Speeds up the information-gathering process.	• Willingness to complete the survey on their own. • Unable to verify understanding.
Survey as the basis for discussion in individual meetings.	Able to clarify understanding.	Time-consuming.

Methods

A. Senior manager completes the survey individually followed by individual meeting.
1. Explain the purpose of the activity to the target group.
2. Give each person a copy of Exercise 17.1 and agree to a time frame for completion.
3. Arrange a follow-up meeting with each person, allowing up to one hour per meeting.
4. Discuss the responses and agree on a development plan.
5. Prepare a development plan, using Exercise 17.2, for the senior manager to communicate to, and win commitment from, their team of managers.

B. Survey as the basis for discussion in individual meetings.
1. Explain the purpose of the activity to the target group.
2. Arrange a meeting with each person, allowing at least two hours per meeting.
3. In each meeting, give the senior manager Exercise 17.1 and ask them to comment on each characteristic in terms of evidence that shows that their team of managers does this. Also ask them which individuals could benefit from improving their performance.
4. Encourage the senior manager to make notes.
5. Close the meeting by agreeing on a development plan for the senior manager's management team.
6. Prepare the development plan, using Exercise 17.2, for the senior manager to communicate to, and win commitment from, their team of managers.

Exercise 17.1: How Do I See My Managers?

Think about the managers in your department. First, for each of the characteristics below, place a checkmark (✓) against those that are in evidence. Second, can you think of someone who could be even more effective if he/she possessed these characteristics? Write the name(s) in the appropriate boxes.

Characteristics	Evident?	Names
Clarifying objectives 1. Put specific problems into context, rather than going into irrelevant detail.		
2. See their own department in terms of the organization as a whole.		
3. Set realistic and achievable objectives that meet organizational goals.		
4. Compare actual results with the objectives set in order to make improvements in the future.		
Planning 1. Gather information to formulate alternatives for action.		
2. Generate useful ideas and suggestions.		
3. Make reasoned decisions.		
4. Develop both short- and long-term plans.		
Communication 1. Listen effectively.		
2. Communicate ideas and thoughts verbally.		
3. Communicate ideas and thoughts in writing.		
4. Select appropriate methods for communicating to all those who need to know.		
Teamwork 1. Motivate their team and individuals.		
2. Involve others in solving problems.		
3. Influence others to gain commitment.		
4. Treat team members according to their individual needs.		
Monitoring 1. Set appropriate standards of work.		
2. Assess performance against the standards.		
3. Give both positive and critical feedback.		
4. Take corrective action at the appropriate time.		

? *Exercise 17.1 (concluded)*

Characteristics	Evident?	Names
Training 1. Identify the training needs of staff.		
2. Plan training to meet these needs.		
3. Provide opportunities for staff to learn.		
4. Assess the effectiveness of training.		
Change 1. See where change is necessary.		
2. Recommend changes that improve effectiveness.		
3. Respond positively to ideas for change.		
4. Create a climate for change within their team.		

158

Reproduced from *Training Needs Analysis Toolkit,* Sharon Bartram and
Brenda Gibson, Gower, Aldershot, 1995

Exercise 17.2: Departmental Development Plan

Team development issue(s)	Plan of action	Time frame

Manager's name	Developmental issue(s)	Plan of action	Time frame

D

Job Skills

This section examines all aspects of people's jobs, with particular reference to knowledge and practical and behavioral skill requirements. It shows where standards are being achieved and where there are shortfalls. There are five activities in this section.

18. Analyzing Jobs
19. Training Needs Survey
20. Task Competencies
21. Working with Others
22. Skills Questionnaire

The target groups are usually all employees, with the exception of senior managers for whom the activities may not be appropriate.

"Analyzing Jobs" is a useful starting point: it helps managers and their staff define the content of jobs which can be the basis for other analysis.

"Training Needs Survey" involves people in taking responsibility for identifying and justifying their own training needs.

"Task Competencies" provides the basis for departmental training records and plans, highlighting the level of skill people have and their flexibility in undertaking a number of tasks.

"Working with Others" explores training needs in the important area of verbal communication.

"Skills Questionnaire" will help you to find out about the knowledge and skills that might be untapped in your organization.

Job skills will usually be part of the role of every trainer. However, before using these activities, ask yourself: "Is this my job?" If your answer is *Yes*, check that you have made the preparations that are necessary to the success of this aspect of training needs analysis. Use the following checklist as your guide.

Preparation	Y	N	Action
Have you 1. Identified and won the support of the appropriate sponsor?			
2. Clarified your objectives — do you know what you want to achieve from using the activity?			
3. Assessed the potential problems of using the activities in this target group and made contingencies for them?			
4. Considered the expectations that taking part will raise, and discussed them with your sponsor and other managers?			
5. Clarified your role? Are you: • facilitating the process? • carrying out the analysis yourself?			
6. Selected the best method of collecting the information from the options given in the activity?			
7. Prepared your presentation for the target group?			

Reproduced from *Training Needs Analysis Toolkit,* Sharon Bartram and
Brenda Gibson, Gower, Aldershot, 1995

18

Analyzing Jobs

Objectives

* To clarify the purpose of jobs.
* To analyze the knowledge and practical skills and behavioral skills required by job holders to perform their jobs.
* To provide a standard to match job holders' performance against.

Description

This activity is an exercise that provides a consistent method for analyzing jobs. When completed, it becomes the basis of further analysis and can be used with the remainder of the activities in this section.

Materials

Sufficient copies of Exercise 18.1.

Collecting Information

Methods	Benefits	Potential problems
Manager completes form for jobs in their department.	Easy to administer.	Limited picture of what tasks are performed within each job.
Training manager/officer interviews experienced job holders and manager to complete analysis.	• Thorough analysis. • Able to compare perceptions of job content. • Consistency throughout organization.	Time to gather information.

163

Methods	Benefits	Potential problems
Manager and experienced job holders complete form for jobs in the department.	• Able to compare perceived job content with actual activities carried out. • Thorough analysis. • Ownership of analysis by department.	Disruption to workplace routine.

Methods

A. Manager completes form for jobs in the department.
1. Explain the purpose of the activity to the target group.
2. Give each manager sufficient copies of Exercise 18.1 and agree on a time frame for completion and return.
3. Maintain an up-to-date record of the content of jobs as the basis of future training needs analysis.

B. Training manager/officer interviews experienced job holders and manager to complete analysis.
1. Explain the purpose of the activity to the target group.
2. Arrange meetings with experienced job holders, allowing up to one hour per meeting.
3. Discuss the content of the job and the requirements, recording their comments on Exercise 18.1.
4. Review the completed analyses with the manager, amending any aspect where necessary.
5. Arrange for the manager to receive copies of the completed Exercise 18.1 to communicate to and win commitment from the job holders.
6. Maintain an up-to-date record of the content of jobs as the basis of future training needs analysis.

C. Manager and experienced job holders complete form for jobs in the department.
1. Explain the purpose of the activity to the target group.
2. Give each manager and job holder sufficient copies of Exercise 18.1 and ensure that they agree on a time to meet together to complete the analysis.
3. Agree on a time frame for the completion and return of the analyses.
4. Maintain an up-to-date record of the content of jobs as the basis of future training needs analysis.

164

Exercise 18.1: Job Analysis

Job Title _____

Task Description _____

_____

Knowledge requirements (what the job holder must know and understand):	1. _____ 2. _____ 3. _____ 4. _____ 5. _____ 6. _____
Practical skill requirements (what the job holder must be able to do and demonstrate):	1. _____ 2. _____ 3. _____ 4. _____ 5. _____ 6. _____
Behavioral skill requirements (how the job holders must conduct themselves with other people):	1. _____ 2. _____ 3. _____ 4. _____ 5. _____ 6. _____

Reproduced from *Training Needs Analysis Toolkit,* Sharon Bartram and
Brenda Gibson, Gower, Aldershot, 1995

19

Training Needs Survey

Objectives

- To generate information from job holders about their perceived training needs in relation to job performance.
- To develop departmental job training plans.
- To identify common training themes across departments.
- To gauge attitudes toward training.

Description

This activity is a short survey that asks the respondents to specify types of training they require in the categories of technical, interpersonal, and information. It can be used in conjunction with Activity 20 to help change attitudes toward training.

Materials

1. Sufficient copies of Exercise 19.1.
2. A meeting room.

Collecting Information

Methods	Benefits	Potential problems
Mailed survey by department.	Easy to administer.	• Low response rate. • Need to follow up.
Short individual interviews by department.	• Needs of all individuals identified. • Able to clarify understanding. • Opportunity to influence attitudes.	• Time-consuming. • Disruption to workplace.

167

Methods

A. Mailed survey by department.
1. Explain the purpose of the activity to the target group.
2. Give each person a copy of Exercise 19.1 and agree on the time frame for completion and return.
3. Summarize the responses.
4. Give a copy of the completed summary to the department manager and agree on a plan of action.
5. Analyze each departmental summary, highlighting common themes, and present a plan of action to all department managers.

B. Short individual interviews by department.
1. Explain the purpose of the activity to the target group.
2. Interview each person, allowing at least 30 minutes per meeting. Discuss the questions on Exercise 19.1 and record the person's responses.

Follow steps 3, 4, and 5 as above.

Exercise 19.1: Training Needs Survey

What training would help me become more effective in my job?

Please specify the type of training you would find most helpful in the given categories.

1. Technical training — relevant to the tasks you perform in your job:

This training will help me in the following ways:

2. Interpersonal skills training — relevant to the interactions you have with people in order to perform your job:

This training will help me in the following ways:

3. Information training — to keep you up to date with new developments and changes that will affect how you perform your job:

This training will help me in the following ways:

NAME _____   JOB TITLE _____

DATE _____   DEPARTMENT _____

169

Reproduced from *Training Needs Analysis Toolkit,* Sharon Bartram and Brenda Gibson, Gower, Aldershot, 1995

20

Task Competencies

Objectives

* To identify gaps in the skill levels of job holders in a department.
* To highlight potential problems of task coverage across a department.

Description

This activity uses a matrix to list all the tasks undertaken in a department and a ranking system to state the current skill levels of job holders across these tasks. Training needs for individuals are then recorded on the matrix along with any task coverage issues that have been highlighted. This activity can be used in conjunction with Activity 19 to develop training plans that have the commitment of managers and job holders.

Materials

Sufficient copies of Exercise 20.1.

Collecting Information

Methods	Benefits	Potential problems
Department manager completes matrix, reports training needs, and proposes actions.	Easy to administer.	• No involvement of job holders. • Less commitment from job holders to training.
Training manager/officer and department manager jointly complete the matrix, identify training needs, and propose actions.	Able to clarify ranking and decisions.	• No involvement of job holders. • Less commitment from job holders to training.

Methods	Benefits	Potential problems
Department manager and job holder jointly complete the matrix, report training needs, and propose actions.	• Dialogue between managers and job holders. • Commitment from job holder and manager for training.	• Disruption to workplace routine.

Methods

A. Department manager completes matrix, reports training needs, and proposes actions.

1. Explain the purpose of the activity to the target group.
2. Give manager sufficient copies of Exercise 20.1 and verify understanding. Explain that individual training needs will be shown by looking across the completed columns, while task coverage issues will be highlighted by looking down the columns. Agree on a time frame for completion and return of exercise.
3. Agree on the training needs and proposed actions, making recommendations as appropriate.

B. Training manager/officer and department manager jointly complete the matrix, identify training needs, and propose actions.

1. Explain the purpose of the activity to the target group.
2. Arrange a meeting with each manager, allowing at least one hour per meeting.
3. During the meeting complete Exercise 20.1, agreeing on training needs and actions.

C. Department manager and job holder jointly complete the matrix, report training needs, and propose actions.

Follow steps 1 and 2 as in the first method.

3. Ensure that managers and job holders set specific dates and times for their meetings. Be available to facilitate these meetings if requested.
4. Agree on the training needs and proposed actions, making recommendations as appropriate.

Exercise 20.1: Task Competencies

DEPARTMENT: _____

Ranking values to indicate skill level:
0 = no experience of this task
1 = being trained in this task
2 = can do this task without supervision
3 = able to train others in this task

NAME	ALL TASKS CARRIED OUT IN THIS DEPARTMENT												ACTION
ACTION REQUIRED? YES/NO													

173

21

Working with Others

Objective

- To identify ways of improving interactions between people, enabling them to increase effectiveness of their job performance.

Description

A pack of cards describing aspects of communication between people is used as a framework for structured discussions with job holders.

Materials

1. Sufficient copies of Exercises 21.1 and 21.3.
2. Exercise 21.2, pasted onto cardboard and then cut into a pack of cards. (3 × 5 index cards, cut in half, can also be used.)
3. A meeting room.

Collecting Information

Method	Benefits	Potential problems
Individual discussions.	Detailed analysis of needs.	Time to complete.

Method

Individual discussions.
1. Explain the purpose of the activity to the target group.
2. Arrange a meeting with each person, allowing at least one hour per meeting.
3. During each meeting give the person a copy of Exercise 21.1 and ask them to first identify those people they work with and write their names on the exercise.

4. Explain that you want them to work through the pack of cards, made from Exercise 21.2, and to answer the three questions on Exercise 21.2 for each person they work with.

5. Use Exercise 21.3 to record relevant information from this discussion. Give a copy of this completed exercise to the person at the end of the meeting.

6. Repeat steps 3, 4, and 5 until all the target group has had a meeting. Use your notes from the exercises to produce a consolidated plan of action. Give feedback to the target group and appropriate managers on the findings.

Exercise 21.1: Who Are They?

Write the names of those people you work with in order to perform your job.

self

subordinates

colleagues, same department

suppliers

manager/supervisor

colleagues, other departments

customers

You will be given a pack of cards, each one describing an aspect of communication between people. One at a time, think about each person you work with and for each card ask yourself these questions:

1. When do I do this?
2. How do I do this?
3. What must I do to improve?

177

Exercise 21.2: Pack of Cards

PERSUADING	INFLUENCING	WINNING AGREEMENT OR COMMITMENT
GAINING INFORMATION FROM	GIVING INFORMATION TO	SAYING *NO*
DISAGREEING	PRESENTING IDEAS	LISTENING
QUESTIONING	STATING PROBLEMS OR DIFFICULTIES	ASKING FOR CLARIFICATION

179

Reproduced from *Training Needs Analysis Toolkit,* Sharon Bartram and
Brenda Gibson, Gower, Aldershot, 1995

Exercise 21.3: Discussion Summary

with _____(name)

_____ (department)

Person	Improvements	Action
Manager:		
Subordinates:		
Colleagues, same department:		
Colleagues, other departments:		
Customers:		
Suppliers:		

22

Skills Questionnaire

Objective

* To generate information about the knowledge and skills individuals possess, which they have gained from previous employment or activities outside the working environment.

Description

This activity is a short questionnaire.

Materials

Sufficient copies of Exercise 22.1.

Collecting Information

Method	Benefits	Potential problems
Mail questionnaire.	Easy to administer.	Low response rate.

Method

Mail questionnaire
1. Explain the purpose of the activity to the target group.
2. Distribute a copy of Exercise 22.1 to each person and agree on a time frame for completion and return.
3. Maintain a record of the completed questionnaire for future reference as part of other training needs analysis activities.

Exercise 22.1: Skills Questionnaire

Name _____   Job title _____

Department _____   Date _____

So that we can develop and better apply your talents in our organization, we would like to know more about you.

1. What academic qualifications do you possess?

2. What professional qualifications do you possess?

3. Are you currently participating in education? If so, what are you studying?

4. Have you received any special awards? What are they?

Life experience

5. Do you possess skills that are not being used in your current job? You may have developed these skills from previous employment in the home, volunteer work, social or community activities. Please describe your skills under these four headings.

Working with information	Working with materials
Working with ideas	Working with people

Please continue on another sheet of paper if necessary.

185

Reproduced from *Training Needs Analysis Toolkit,* Sharon Bartram and Brenda Gibson, Gower, Aldershot, 1995